SUCCULENT OBSESSION

SUCCULENT
OBSESSION
A COMPLETE GUIDE

KEN SHELF   PHOTOGRAPHY BY RACHEL WEILL

ROCKRIDGE
PRESS

For general information on our other products and services or to obtain technical support, please contact our Customer Care Department within the United States at (866) 744-2665, or outside the United States at (510) 253-0500.

Rockridge Press publishes its books in a variety of electronic and print formats. Some content that appears in print may not be available in electronic books, and vice versa.

Interior and Cover Designer: Lisa Schreiber
Art Producer: Samantha Ulban
Editor: Georgia Freedman
Production Editor: Dylan Julian
Production Manager: Riley Hoffman

Photography © 2021 Rachel Weill. Photos taken at Succulence in San Francisco, California.

Hardcover ISBN: 978-1-68539-701-2 | eBook ISBN: 978-1-63807-856-2
R0

For Marble,
who helps us weather the storm

CONTENTS

INTRODUCTION

The shared love of succulents creates a camaraderie among strangers. The internet has provided a forum where we can post pictures, ask questions, trade cuttings, and share in a community of like-minded individuals. As we dive deeper into this world, our love for **succulents** (see Glossary, page 237) grows ever stronger. Over the last 10 years, the globalization of this trend means more wild succulent varieties traveling to every corner of the earth. What once was unobtainable now lands on our front steps within days. A quest for new plants can send us all over the web and to every plant store within a day's drive. Yes, our collective drive for succulent plant knowledge has become an obsession. At my shop, Succulence, we see it in our customers. We see it in ourselves.

In the few short years since I wrote my first book, *Essential Succulents: The Beginner's Guide,* I have watched a cottage industry become an international phenomenon. And that was before the pandemic. Once we found ourselves at home all the time, our desire to fill our spaces with plants went through the roof. In San Francisco, where I live, new plant stores have bloomed in every neighborhood at the same time that other retail stores have closed. People's passion for plants has become an obsession—and their succulent collection a source of perpetual pride.

At my store, we shifted our business model to allow for virtual shopping and virtual workshops, and suddenly we were making plant art with people in Chicago, New York, Boston, and Washington, DC, and meeting new customers all over the country. There is nothing quite so remarkable as shipping a haworthia across the country to a private home in South Carolina so that we can meet online and plant a **vertical garden** (see Glossary, page 237) together with a group of far-flung friends or colleagues.

Although my staff and I were dismayed by the health crisis, we found solace and even joy in being able to connect with an ever-widening base of succulent fans, something we never imagined at the beginning.

And we learned about you. We learned that you had an unquenchable thirst for knowledge about your plants. *What type is it?* you wanted to know. *What varietal? How do I nurture it? How do I propagate it, and when? How do I care for it and protect it from harm? How do I show it all this love I feel?* These are such relatable questions and the same ones I am always asking myself. No matter what your level of personal expertise, there are always going to be new plants to learn about and new techniques to care for those plants. I conceived of and wrote this book with this in mind, to help you care for and identify the plants you have and to arm you with the knowledge to care for your future plants as well.

In the following pages I share details about 100 easy-to-grow succulent plants, most of which you can get at your local nursery and all of which are easily available in the online marketplace. I share information about caring for these plants indoors and outdoors, as well as designing with them. I also offer you an easy-to-follow, step-by-step guide to diagnosing and treating the common problems that everyone faces as they help their plants grow and thrive. I recognize that we all, amateurs and experienced gardeners alike, dream of having the most perfect, Instagram-ready plants on earth and feeling the pride that comes with caring for those plants and sharing them with our friends. I want to nurture that pride. And I want to help you all grow into lifelong plant lovers who feel confident and knowledgeable about their plants and how to maintain them.

Chapter 1

100 EASY-CARE SUCCULENTS AND CACTI

Succulents have evolved all over the planet, from the southern tip of Africa to the mountains of Peru. With the proper light and water, you can grow and enjoy them no matter where you live. Although they have evolved to be self-reliant in many harsh climates, many can adapt to indoor houseplant life. As landscape greenery, succulents use less water than other plant varieties and provide bold, artistic imagery for you and your neighbors. They are also excellent housemates, not needing much more than a passing hello every week or two and providing you with steady companionship and, occasionally, pretty flowers. Succulents are great plants to grow and admire, but their value doesn't end there. Some are made into beverages and eaten as food; some are used as medicines or for fire safety.

In this chapter, you'll find a collection of 100 easy-to-grow, easy-to-find hardy succulents that can thrive in a variety of regions. I want your confidence and skill level to grow along with them, so here you'll find lots of information for each plant, including seasonal information about when your plant will bloom, when it might be **dormant**, and when and how to **propagate** it (see Glossary, page 237). Paired with knowledge of your indoor and outdoor environments, this guide will provide all you need to choose the proper plants for any growing situation. Scan the guide to determine what's appropriate based on your hardiness zone, where you will be planting, and how much sun and water the plants will need. I've also provided facts about each plant's geographic origins, tips for cultivation, and a variety of challenges to watch out for. My goal is to get you as excited about succulents as I am. Follow these instructions, and don't be afraid to experiment. Sometimes you learn from things that don't work out. The important thing is to enjoy the process. Ritualize your plant care. Don't rush it. Look at each plant carefully. Notice any changes, such as new growth or problematic leaves. Enjoy this special time. It is your time. These are your plants. This is your life. Your succulent lifestyle awaits.

SUCCULENT BASICS

Succulents don't require a whole lot of care. Though it may seem counterintuitive, they are actually stronger when neglected. It is easy to "overcare" for them by providing too much water or fertilizer. There are some variations in the care required for these plants, but many general rules apply. Familiarize yourself with the following basic guidelines, and you'll soon become a confident succulent cultivator. (We will go into greater detail on care in chapter 2.)

Watering can be kept to a minimum. Many succulent families emerged in areas of extreme drought and can exist for long periods in that state. In general, succulents would much rather be underwatered than overwatered. Container gardens, including any plants that are not planted directly in the ground, need to be watered by hand or through an irrigation system. Plants in the earth will start taking pretty good care of themselves by the time they are large enough to fit in six-inch nursery pots. Smaller plants may need regular water until they are established.

Fertilization can be required if your plant is in older or non-augmented soil, but it is not needed often. A great attribute of succulents is their ability to withstand neglect. While other types of plants appreciate food—and at times need it to continue to thrive—succulents evolved to take care of themselves. There is a term we use to describe the pretty colors that appear when succulents get extra sun, cold, or heat combined with a lack of water

and fertilizer: *stress*. A good rule of thumb is to feed succulents during the warm growth months that usually stretch from early spring through late fall, though some plants will grow in the colder months. An example of a winter-growing succulent is the aeonium, which is dormant in summer.

Pruning and manicuring need occur only when you want to trim for appearance or propagation (see the next paragraph). In some cases, growth may be stunted when there are many branches on a plant, and that might be a time to prune. Manicuring means pruning for shape. This cutting can be accomplished by pinching off bits with your fingers or a sharp pair of garden scissors below the rosette or set of leaves where the stem connects to a branch. An aeonium or aloe might require larger tools, such as shears or clippers. Euphorbias secrete a toxic sap, so wear gloves when pruning those plants.

Propagation is when you grow new plants from an existing one. This is part of the fun of succulents, which can often regrow themselves from just one leaf. Many of the plant families propagate differently, through leaves, cuttings, offsets, or division. Try propagation when you want more plants for your home, gifts for friends, cuttings for plant art, or to clear the plant of excessive growth. You can also compost extra pieces that you don't use. See chapter 4 for specific propagation instructions.

Acclimation is an important part of caring for a young plant or transferring any plant from indoors to outdoors. Succulents need to be slowly acclimated to bright light if they have spent months inside. Give them a little more light each day for a week or two before leaving them out in the heat completely.

Now let's take an in-depth look at some of our favorite, easy-to-grow succulents:

KEY LIME PIE
AKA CRINKLE LEAF PLANT
Adromischus cristatus

HARDINESS ZONE AND TEMPERATURE RANGE
9–10; 20°F–90°F

IDEAL LIGHTING
Full sun to partial shade

GROWING LOCATION
Outdoors/indoors

MATURE SIZE
4–6" tall

PROPAGATION
Leaf: get a clean cut to prevent rot; don't water until new leaves appear, soon after new roots

This South African native has whimsical, plump, triangular leaves that look like a pinched-off pie crust at the top. They are covered in tiny white hairs, giving the plant a soft and fuzzy look. A slow grower, Key Lime Pie will never get very large, and it won't be very needy either.

Special Features: Similar to haworthia, Key Lime Pie sends its flowers out on a long stem in the spring. The flower is tubular and white with reddish tips. Although it doesn't have a fragrance, it has a pretty star shape; the flowers frequently bloom in batches.

Care Instructions: Key Lime Pie is about as easy as it gets in the succulent world. Water when it's fully dry and keep it in bright light indoors, and it should reward you for a few months a year with its flowers. When growing outdoors, it needs partial sun and no frost.

Watch Out For: Mealybugs and weevils have been known to attack this plant. They are controllable with any basic pesticide. Good air circulation will help with overall health.

Arrangement Tips: Because of its size, this succulent is great on an office desk or on your windowsill. It is also fantastic as a counter shape in planters with echeveria, graptopetalum, and other small rosette succulents. It makes a nice little dining table plant, leaving plenty of room for your salad bowl.

BLACK ROSE

AKA BLACK BEAUTY, PURPLE CREST AEONIUM

Aeonium arboreum 'Zwartkop'

HARDINESS ZONE AND TEMPERATURE RANGE
9–11; 25°F–100°F

IDEAL LIGHTING
Full sun to partial shade

GROWING LOCATION
Outdoors

MATURE SIZE
1–6' tall; 2–3' spread

PROPAGATION
Stem cutting, branch; winter

This aeonium has shiny 6- to 8-inch rosettes that are a waxy deep burgundy to black atop thin bare stems. All aeoniums are native to North Africa and the Canary Islands. This one will be darker and more striking in fuller sun and will have a green center with purplish leaves in full shade.

Special Features: Although this plant is **monocarpic** (it flowers, then dies; see Glossary, page 237), when it goes into bloom, it is an extraordinary display, sending a huge conical growth covered in hundreds of yellow flowers from the center of a single rosette. Flowers will last longer than a month and keep your attention the entire time. The branch that blooms will die, but the plant may have many branches that bloom at different times or during different years.

Care Instructions: Zwartkop goes mostly dormant in the summer. It likes moderate water during the winter growing months and can take a bit more heat than its other aeonium family members.

Watch Out For: Sometimes this plant will drop leaves during the dormant months as it focuses its energy on its stems and roots. Water monthly during this time to keep it fully hydrated. Keep an eye out for mealybugs and spider mites. Zwartkop is said to be deer-resistant.

Arrangement Tips: Black rose is great as a **specimen plant** (see Glossary, page 237). It's terrific in containers with cactus and sedum or as a stand-alone plant. Contrast it with *Echeveria imbricata* and *Sedum* 'Red Robin', or go all in with dark plants like *Echeveria* 'Black Prince', *Sedum spathulifolium* 'Purpureum' (page 185) and *Sedum* 'Vera Jameson'.

AEONIUM 'KIWI'

Aeonium 'Kiwi'

HARDINESS ZONE AND TEMPERATURE RANGE
9–11; 30°F–75°F

IDEAL LIGHTING
Partial sun
to full sun

GROWING LOCATION
Outdoors

MATURE SIZE
2–3' tall; 1–2' spread

PROPAGATION
Stem cuttings,
branch; winter

The Kiwi has thick, fleshy oval-shaped leaves with pointed tips. Its leaves tend to be a yellowish lime green in the center and get greener heading toward their bright pinkish-red edges.

Special Features: The coloration on the leaves will become more pronounced with sun exposure. This aeonium also makes gorgeous yellow blooms in late spring or summer. It is a monocarpic plant, meaning it will flower once and then die. However, the rosettes may not bloom at the same time, and there is plenty of time to propagate this plant by stem cuttings.

Care Instructions: Water kiwi regularly when first planting; change to occasional watering once it's established. In the summer, water just when there is very dry heat, and in the winter, water monthly. Aeoniums will frequently be dormant in the summer and won't need much to drink during that time if the temperature is mild.

Watch Out For: Don't let this plant sit in water, as it is prone to root rot. It is also prone to sunburn and would prefer partial shade in a hotter climate. Sunburned leaves will turn brown and fall off. This won't kill the plant, but it won't look great until it grows new leaves.

Arrangement Tips: This variety looks great in rock gardens, as a specimen, with companions such as Blue Senecio, or with sedums such as Cape Blanco (page 185) and Coppertone Stonecrop (page 181).

A Note About Aeoniums: While some people suggest aeoniums as a great indoor plant, my experience suggests they prefer to be outside, where they get a regular flow of air and feel the direct sunlight on their stems and branches. This contributes to the general health and elasticity of these plants.

MARDI GRAS

Aeonium 'Mardi Gras'

HARDINESS ZONE AND TEMPERATURE RANGE
9-11; 25°F-85°F

IDEAL LIGHTING
Full sun to
partial sun

GROWING LOCATION
Outdoors/indoors

MATURE SIZE
12" tall; 36" spread

PROPAGATION
Stem cutting,
year-round;
leaf, winter

This is a striking aeonium, with coloring that changes with the seasons and with sun exposure. It's named after the wild colors of the Mardi Gras festival, and the name suits the plant: the green and yellows toward the center are flanked by reds that can become the brightest magenta all the way out to the outer leaves of the rosette. Like all aeoniums, Mardi Gras is monocarpic, meaning it produces one flower, which then brings death to the rosette that bloomed her.

Special Features: Mardi Gras's color makes them popular in a variety of garden settings. They're also easy to plant from cuttings; in California's Bay Area (where I live), you can just stick a branch into soil any time of year and it will flourish.

Care Instructions: In summer, the rosettes close up a bit, as they become dormant. They don't need much water during this time, just a monthly soak. If you can shade them a bit in the summer, they will thank you by not going fully into dormancy. In winter, the rosettes will open up wide. New branches and rosettes will arrive during winter and spring. In theory, this is when flowers also arrive, but I have never seen Mardi Gras bloom, indoors or outdoors.

Watch Out For: Make sure not to overwater in the summer. Make sure your aeonium doesn't walk away—when these plants get larger, they send out aerial roots from the stem to the ground, making it look like the plant is up on tiptoes. When growing indoors, make sure the light is strong and they get some air circulation, which will help them maintain elasticity and not get too brittle.

Arrangement Tips: The concentric leaves of the Mardi Gras look like flowers, so planting them in a planter in a bright spot in your home will be like have a bouquet of aeonium all year.

SUNBURST

AKA COPPER PINWHEEL

Aeonium 'Sunburst'

HARDINESS ZONE
AND TEMPERATURE
RANGE
9–11; 30°F–85°F

IDEAL LIGHTING
Full sun to
partial shade

GROWING
LOCATION
Outdoors

MATURE SIZE
1½–2' tall;
1½–2' wide

PROPAGATION
Stem cutting,
branch; winter

This showy aeonium has enormous rosettes that span up to 16 inches across, with a variety of different colors. The leaves can be bright yellow with varying thicknesses of green center striping, changing in size around each rosette. They can also be a creamier white with thick strips of **variegated** green (see Glossary, page 237), like a brushstroke that hasn't been smoothed out, and pink coloring on the edges. Sunburst is native to North Africa and the Canary Islands.

Special Features: This plant, like all aeoniums, is monocarpic, with white or yellow flower cones in spring, summer, and sometimes winter.

Care Instructions: This plant is drought-tolerant and can withstand very little water in the dormant summer if the weather is temperate.

Watch Out For: Curling of the leaves can suggest the plant is due for a good drink of water. It is prone to sunburn in high heat.

Arrangement Tips: Sunburst looks great in rock gardens or containers. Plant it with *Aeonium* 'Zwartkop' (page 6), which has similar needs, or as a visual counterpoint to *Agave attenuata* 'Kara's Stripe' (page 17) or Parry's Agave (page 18). It also looks dramatic with chunky lava rocks underneath an aloe tree.

CENTURY PLANT, WHITE-STRIPED CENTURY PLANT

Agave americana 'Mediopicta alba'

HARDINESS ZONE AND TEMPERATURE RANGE
8–11; 15°F–80°F

IDEAL LIGHTING
Full sun to partial shade

GROWING LOCATION
Outdoors/indoors

MATURE SIZE
5' tall; 5' spread

PROPAGATION
Offsets: year-round

This varietal of *Agave americana* has an amazing variegation. Its thick leaves are bluish green along the spiny margins with a thick creamy-white stripe going up the center all the way out to the terminal spine at the tip. The spines on the agave are no joke, so use care when handling them. The plant can be small when you first get it and can live happily inside your house with bright full sun for five years as it grows.

Special Features: Like most agaves, this monocarpic plant sends out a variegated stem that can grow 15 feet or taller! The blooms are white and yellow, and hummingbirds will linger around them for a long time until they dry. These plants don't flower until they are at least 10 years old, and sometimes not for more than 30 years. They are called Century Plants because, I guess, we like to exaggerate.

Care Instructions: Agave are pretty simple. They need a lot of sun and not a ton of water. They are a classic neglect plant if they are outside. Inside, they still need some water but not very much. Water every three weeks or so, as long as the sun exposure is bright and regular.

Watch Out For: Those spines! They can really hurt. But if you can respect your agave's space, it will look fantastic and is well worth living with. Just give it a spot where people don't have to engage with it except to water.

Arrangement Tips: Inside, place your Century Plant by the window and enjoy its pretty coloration. Outside, plant it on hillsides, as borders, and in raised beds in your yard.

VARIEGATED FOX TAIL AGAVE

Agave attenuata 'Kara's Stripes'

HARDINESS ZONE AND TEMPERATURE RANGE
10-12: down to 35°F

IDEAL LIGHTING
Full sun, partial sun, full shade

GROWING LOCATION
Outdoors

MATURE SIZE
2-4' tall; 3-6' spread

PROPAGATION
Offsets: year-round

This agave's translucent yellowish-green leaves form soft rosettes that tilt slightly upward toward the sky, as if looking into the sun. *Agave attenuata* is native to Mexico.

Special Features: Thought to be a slow grower, Variegated Fox Tail will live for around 20 years, at which point the monocarpic plant will send up its 10- to 15-foot flower stalk and finish its life in a show of fragrant yellow-green flowers. The stalk, unlike the straight asparagus shape of many other agave plants, frequently bends over and dips down, forming an arch.

Care Instructions: There is little to do for this easy agave. It is frost-sensitive, so cover it with frost cloth during a cold spell. It is heat-tolerant but would love some afternoon shade if the temperature is very warm, so plant accordingly.

Watch Out For: Overwatering is a concern. In general, it won't need any water during the dormant winter months.

Arrangement Tips: Its bright, colorful appearance, which will improve in good sun, makes it a crowd-pleaser in any garden setting. It would be majestic planted alone in a wine barrel planter. Alongside sedums and aeoniums, it will be a point of focus. Variegated Fox Tail will help delineate spaces when planted along fences with aloes and other agaves.

PARRY'S AGAVE
AKA ARTICHOKE AGAVE
Agave parryi var. huachucensis

HARDINESS ZONE AND TEMPERATURE RANGE
5–11: known to survive cold temperatures down to -20°F

IDEAL LIGHTING
Full sun to filtered sun

GROWING LOCATION
Outdoors

MATURE SIZE
2' by 2', with a flowering stalk that can reach 15' tall

PROPAGATION
Offsets: spring and summer

An agave native to Mexico and the southwest United States, this plant will take 10 to 20 years to attain full growth, at which point it flowers magnificently and then dies.

Special Features: Parry's Agave has very pretty grayish-blue leaves with sharp teeth along the spine of each leaf and a sharp spine on the end. The top of the leaf will have a brownish color. When the plant flowers, it will send a large treelike stalk from the center of the plant that eventually forms 20 to 30 branches, each with a large cluster of yellow flowers. The fermented pulp of this plant can be distilled to make mezcal and tequila.

Care Instructions: This plant requires very little care outdoors; once established, it will not need to be watered. It cannot be propagated with leaves, but you can collect offsets somewhat regularly.

Watch Out For: Watch out for scale, a bug that attaches itself to the underside of plant leaves; this can be treated with an insecticidal soap or a neem oil spray. Parry's Agave also must have a gritty, sandy planting mix or it can form root rot.

Arrangement Tips: Because Parry's Agave is such a hardy plant, it makes a great landscape pick in wintry areas. Plant it in groupings with about 3 feet of space between each one.

QUEEN VICTORIA AGAVE

Agave victoriae-reginae

**HARDINESS ZONE
AND TEMPERATURE
RANGE**
9–11; 15°F–90°F

IDEAL LIGHTING
Full sun

**GROWING
LOCATION**
Outdoors/indoors:
must have great
sun indoors

MATURE SIZE
18" tall by 18" wide

PROPAGATION
Offsets: year-round

Compact dark green rosettes with intricate white markings make this a very showy plant. It's ideal as a specimen or isolated with boulders and only smaller plants around it. Most varieties do not have marginal teeth on the leaves but do have a 1- to 3-inch thorn at the end of each leaf. It is native to Mexico.

Special Features: Like most agaves, Queen Victoria will bloom once after 10 to 25 years with a thick stalk covered in dense greenish-white flowers tinged with purples and reds.

Care Instructions: Queen Victoria Agave loves a gritty, well-draining soil. Water it about once a month inside, when dry. Outside, water rarely—only once a month during hot seasons and not at all during the winter. It loves the heat but is also very hardy in the cold. Propagate it by removing offsets. The plant will also give you seedpods when the flower is done; allow the pods to dry before opening and removing the seeds.

Watch Out For: Use caution when dealing with agaves. Although this one does not have marginal teeth, the spikes on the ends of each leaf will leave a painful reminder if you get poked. Use gloves, and wear long pants and solid shoes when transplanting. It is mostly pest-free, but, as with most agaves, look for scale and treat immediately.

Arrangement Tips: Put this agave in a planter at your front door or in a living room high off the ground where no one can poke themselves on it. Set it around boulders in a yard but not with other large shrubs that can obscure it from view. Plant low succulents of solid blues and oranges around it to show off its pretty markings.

FRIZZLE SIZZLE

AKA CORKSCREW ALBUCA

Albuca spiralis

HARDINESS ZONE AND TEMPERATURE RANGE
8–10; 60°F–85°F

IDEAL LIGHTING
Full sun to partial sun

GROWING LOCATION
Outdoors/indoors

MATURE SIZE
24" tall

PROPAGATION
Offsets: winter grow months

We're obsessed with the shape of Frizzle Sizzle! It has a little **caudex** (the exposed root ball above the soil; see Glossary, page 237), which looks a lot like an onion with curly green leaves rising up from the center. The leaves are ridiculous and look like ribbons made in a factory. (Thank you, nature!) It is a winter grower and features sweet vanilla-smelling yellow flowers; each dangles from a single stalk.

Special Features: Frizzle Sizzle's flowers bloom off a large stalk that emerges from the center of the plant. The buds are large and bulbous. Although they are pretty and smell good, they hasten the dropping of the phantasmagorical leaves, so some people remove the buds before they even open. The curly leaves will be thicker with more sun.

Care Instructions: Water weekly during the winter grow months, before the soil is fully dried out. During summer dormancy, stop watering until new foliage starts to grow. Remove the buds when they emerge to avoid browning the tips of the leaves, if you value them over the flowers. Your Albuca doesn't love the hottest light, nor does it love hot or cold air blowing around it. Find it a nice spot where it will get bright light and mostly still air and, of course, where it will get admired.

Watch Out For: Don't overreact when Frizzle Sizzle loses all its leaves during the late spring and summer; they will turn brown and fall off, then grow back during the winter months. *Albuca spiralis* has almost no pest issues at all, so as long as you nurse the caudex all year, it will live for a long time.

Arrangement Tips: Keep this one in its own pretty, handmade ceramic pot with great drainage. Put it somewhere you like to sit so you can admire it when the leaves are full.

ALOE VERA

Aloe barbadensis

HARDINESS ZONE AND TEMPERATURE RANGE
10-11: down to 35°F-40°F

IDEAL LIGHTING
Full sun, partial sun, partial shade

GROWING LOCATION
Outdoors/indoors

MATURE SIZE
1-2' tall: 2-3' wide

PROPAGATION
Offsets, root division: spring and summer

Humans have been using Aloe Vera for skincare and in cosmetics for at least 2,000 years. It is native to the Arabian Peninsula but grows in the wild all over the planet. It is an easy plant to grow inside or outside. It makes long, tubular yellow-green flowers but usually only when grown outdoors.

Special Features: The sap of the thick leaves of this aloe is a great treatment for burns and light abrasions, making it a popular houseplant among parents.

Care Instructions: Outdoors this is a drought-tolerant plant that needs little care. Give it some irrigation during the hottest months and less during the winter. Indoors, water moderately, also tapering off during winter. It propagates most easily through the division of offsets, which will pop up either right next to the plant or a few inches away. To keep a container plant happy, be sure to remove and replant the offsets every three or four years.

Watch Out For: Scale and mealybugs are possibilities. Though Aloe Vera has a beautiful flower, it rarely blooms as an indoor plant. Brown tips on your leaves can be a sign of not enough water, and black tips can mean too much water. If you live somewhere that's cold in the winter, bring this plant outside in the spring, but be careful to acclimate it slowly to the sun, as it is surprisingly prone to sunburn. Sunburned leaves won't kill the plant, but the damage won't go away until it makes new leaves.

Arrangement Tips: Outside, this is a great border plant, and it will look especially nice in rock gardens and around boulders. Inside, it will provide height in small container gardens and will also look lovely alone in a terra-cotta pot on the kitchen windowsill.

ALOE BLUE ELF

AKA ALOE CALIFORNIA

Aloe 'Blue Elf'

HARDINESS ZONE AND TEMPERATURE RANGE
9–11; 20°F–100°F

IDEAL LIGHTING
Full sun, partial shade

GROWING LOCATION
Outdoors/indoors

MATURE SIZE
12–18" tall; 2' spread

PROPAGATION
Root division, offsets; spring

A **clumping** aloe (see Glossary, page 237) that can live in extreme heat, Aloe Blue Elf has straight-standing grayish-blue leaves and creates a spike of orange flowers throughout winter that can be tinged with red in very hot climates. It has been known to flower intermittently all year long.

Special Features: This aloe has elegant foliage; its ability to withstand heat and drought make it a fabulous landscaping plant. No one knows exactly where it comes from. Aloes are native to the African continent, and some experts think the Blue Elf originated in South Africa, but others say it was farther north, possibly on the Canary or Cape Verde Islands.

Care Instructions: Outdoors, this succulent needs only intermittent water during the hottest months. Indoors, water it every two weeks or when the soil is dry. When the Blue Elf is not getting as much sun as it wants, its foliage will turn greener, and it may not flower.

Watch Out For: Aloe Blue Elf is not prone to many pests or diseases. Don't plant it under trees, which can drop pest-ridden foliage onto the leaves. If the leaves are yellowing or drying at the tips, use a high-phosphate fertilizer in the early winter to promote those gorgeous blooms. Don't forget to prune the stalks when they are done flowering.

Arrangement Tips: If you have lots of space, this can be a great ground cover, as it's known to create a ton of offsets and clump beautifully. It looks stunning when an entire patch is in bloom, and it attracts hummingbirds and other garden life.

PINK BLUSH ALOE

Aloe 'Pink Blush'

HARDINESS ZONE AND TEMPERATURE RANGE
9-11; 40°F-80°F

IDEAL LIGHTING
Full sun to partial shade

GROWING LOCATION
Indoors

MATURE SIZE
12" tall

PROPAGATION
Offsets: year-round

This easy-to-grow aloe plant has delightful green-white-and-pink-tinged leaves. Raised white and pink markings almost look like digital art, and there are bright pink teeth on the margins of the leaves! This is one of a batch of small aloe hybrids created by Kelly Griffin, a succulent breeder who specializes in aloes and agaves.

Special Features: This aloe's flowers emerge off short, thin spikes in late winter and early spring. They are tubular flowers of orange and yellow and red, and they are known to attract hummingbirds.

Care Instructions: When you give your pink blush lots of great, strong light, the colors will intensify with the brightness. The leaves are brittle and liable to break off easily, so handle this plant as little as possible. If you do accidentally break off a leaf, let it callous and give leaf propagation a shot. (It's not easy, but you have nothing to lose.)

Watch Out For: Pink Blush Aloe is a slow grower; try not to be impatient. You may never need to transplant this aloe. While it is in danger of root rot, it does not attract the usual pests, making it an ideal houseplant.

Arrangement Tips: This is a great container garden plant, as it will highlight so many other colors and textures. It will look great in your rock garden around larger plants, such as agaves, that share a similar shape. It will also be just fine by itself in a container by your window.

FAN ALOE

Aloe plicatilis or *Kumara plicatilis*

HARDINESS ZONE AND TEMPERATURE RANGE
9–11; down to 20°F–25°F

IDEAL LIGHTING
Full sun to partial sun

GROWING LOCATION
Outdoors/indoors

MATURE SIZE
Typically grows to 4–8' tall and spreads 4–6' wide, but known to grow up to 16' tall in the wild.

PROPAGATION
Stem cuttings, branch; year-round

Plicatilis is a Latin term meaning "foldable" or "pleated." The leaves of this plant don't fold, but they do look like an extended fan. The plant will typically grow like a tree or a **caudiciform**-like shrub (see Glossary, page 237), with a bulbous base above the soil and a barky gray trunk rising from the ground. Native to South Africa, this fascinating aloe sends out sets of blue-gray leaves that curve into one another.

Special Features: This aloe's leaves are attractive and with full sun can be translucent at the tips, glowing a reddish orange. The Fan Aloe's tubular red flowers will typically bloom between spring and fall in the United States, but they can also appear in the other seasons. The bark is quite fire-resistant, so it is a good plant for dry regions prone to wildfires.

Care Instructions: Outdoors it will want water in the winter and early spring, so irrigate if you live in a drier climate. Indoors it will need as much brightness as possible. The leaves will naturally turn black and fall off, revealing the smooth young bark below. However, inside, if your leaves are turning mushy before turning black, this could mean your plant is not getting enough light or is getting too much water with not enough drainage. It is a slow grower both outdoors or indoors, and it is easily propagated through stem or branch cuttings (remember to let them dry before replanting).

Watch Out For: Root rot from wet soil can be a problem here, as can mealybugs and scale, which can be treated with a neem oil–based spray.

Arrangement Tips: The Fan Aloe's fancy shape makes it a remarkable plant, so it will look elegant wherever you place it. It is great in large decorative containers, with agaves and senecios as companions. It looks fantastic as part of any outdoor landscaping, especially when its tubular blooms are in full swing.

SAND ROSE

Anacampseros rufescens

HARDINESS ZONE AND TEMPERATURE RANGE
10-11: down to 25°F

IDEAL LIGHTING
Full sun to partial shade

GROWING LOCATION
Outdoors/indoors

MATURE SIZE
3-4" tall; 4-6" spread

PROPAGATION
Offsets; year-round

Native to southern Africa, this small clumping plant can get lush colors in full sun. Its botanical name is very old and has been used to describe different plants for hundreds of years, including herbs used to lure lost love homeward. It flowers in the spring, but unless it is a bright, sunny day of at least 85°F, the long maroon buds probably won't open. The flowers can be pink, purple, or violet.

Special Features: The leaves are triangular, with green on most tops and pinks and purples on the bottom. The leaves are also spaced close together on the stems, and the plant appears a little jiggly as it flops one way or the other. There are delicate hairs all over the stems and leaves of this plant.

Care Instructions: Sand Rose is very easy to propagate from seed. Water it only when dry. Bring this drought-tolerant plant inside in cold climates; it will die from frost.

Watch Out For: Mealybugs and aphids can be a problem. Treat accordingly.

Arrangement Tips: This plant's interesting coloring makes it a favorite in container gardens, next to a small sedum or with *Senecio* 'Fishhooks' (page 197) crawling across the soil around it. Place all that in front of a tall aeonium for a vibrant display.

RED APPLE

Aptenia cordifolia

HARDINESS ZONE AND TEMPERATURE RANGE
9-12; 40°F-80°F

IDEAL LIGHTING
Full sun to partial sun

GROWING LOCATION
Outdoors/indoors

MATURE SIZE
1-3" tall;
18-24" spread

PROPAGATION
Root division, stem cuttings; year-round

Aptenia has fleshy green, heart- and oval-shaped leaves with a fast-growing root system that fans out to form a carpet of ground cover. It is native to southern Africa.

Special Features: Red Apple explodes with daisylike flowers bursting throughout the plant in pink, red, purple, yellow, or white. The flowers open during the bright hours and close at night. In some areas, it is used medicinally as an anti-inflammatory, poultice, and deodorant. It's also known as a love charm.

Care Instructions: Water this plant only when it's dry. You won't need fertilizer as this plant will grow strong even if it's never watered. Trim it for shape, as needed or desired, using sharp pruners. It can be immediately replanted in other beds or containers. If it is in a container, bring it inside when the temperature drops below 40°F.

Watch Out For: Red Apple is prone to root rot, so plant it in gritty, very well-draining soil. Water it very lightly, if at all, in the winter. Aptenia has a tendency to climb around other plants, so if you plant it near trees, keep it trimmed around the base. Weed regularly.

Arrangement Tips: With its sparkling flowers, this is lovely ground cover. It's also great for soil erosion control on a hill or slope and terrific in tree wells and along paths.

BISHOP'S CAP CACTUS
AKA BISHOP'S HAT OR STAR CACTUS
Astrophytum myriostigma

HARDINESS ZONE AND TEMPERATURE RANGE
9–11; 25°F–75°F

IDEAL LIGHTING
Partial sun to partial shade

GROWING LOCATION
Outdoors/indoors

MATURE SIZE
40" tall

PROPAGATION
Seeds: spring and summer

The Latin meaning of *Astrophytum* is "star plant," and it is aptly named; its three to seven ribs give it a starlike appearance from above. This spineless Mexican mountain cactus is relatively spherical in its first few years and grows more oblong over time. It develops tiny white dots all over its flesh called trichomes. The top of this slow grower also has a few tufts of grayish silver hair.

Special Features: Outdoors, *Astrophytum* will bloom in the spring, but indoors, the flowers generally appear in summer. They are small and fragrant and can be white or yellow with a center that may be orange, yellow, or red. Each flower lasts only about two days, but the cactus may bloom continuously for a few months. Collect the dry flowers for the seeds.

Care Instructions: Bishop's Cap requires winter rest, meaning less water and a cooler environment. Start withholding some water in autumn and stop completely during the winter. Start up again with small amounts of moisture when the weather starts getting warmer. Spread some sand over the base of your *Astrophytum* to protect it against pests. It doesn't like humidity, so keep it out of the bathroom.

Watch Out For: Mealybugs and scale can be problems for this cactus. Don't worry if your Bishop's Cap takes a while to bloom; you aren't doing anything wrong. Although it might flower after just a few years, flowering could also take up to five or six years.

Arrangement Tips: If you live where you can have this cactus outdoors, plant it under taller shrubbery so that you can enjoy a slightly early flowering season. Inside, keep it near a window and pair it with other plants with the same winter dormancy, or give it a pretty pot and admire it alone.

PONYTAIL PALM
AKA ELEPHANT'S FOOT
Beaucarnea recurvata

HARDINESS ZONE AND TEMPERATURE RANGE
10–11; 15°F–85°F

IDEAL LIGHTING
Full sun to partial sun

GROWING LOCATION
Outdoors/indoors

MATURE SIZE
8' inside, 25' outside

PROPAGATION
Offsets; year-round

Ponytail palm is, guess what? Not a palm! It is a succulent with family roots similar to agave plants. It is a caudex succulent, with a fat stem at the soil level that holds water, making this a drought-tolerant, hardy plant. The stem narrows and grows tall, and long green cascading leaves spill out of the top, looking like fireworks tumbling back to earth. This plant is native to Mexico where it gets hot, full sun, so don't be afraid to give it lots of light.

Special Features: In spring and summer, large, older specimens may bloom in giant splashes of purple or yellow or red above the foliage. You will notice a large spike emerge from the top of the plant, and the feathery spike will produce lots of small branches containing hundreds of tiny blooms. The Ponytail Palm hardly ever blooms inside.

Care Instructions: Treat this plant like you would a cactus. Water it a couple times a month in the spring and summer, and reduce that nearly in half during the fall and winter. If you fertilize, go easy, because too much mineral buildup can result in brown leaf tips. This plant is a slow grower and may stay reasonably small for 5 to 10 years.

Watch Out For: Mealybugs, scale, and aphids are problematic for this plant. Don't forget that this is a succulent and doesn't want to be overwatered. If it has a dish beneath the pot, always empty it after the water drains.

Arrangement Tips: If you are lucky enough to live in the right climate to grow your Ponytail Palm outside, let this become a tree! Inside, put it on a shelf or hang it in a window when it is small, then give it a central spot in your brightest room when it starts to get large.

STRING OF HEARTS

Ceropegia woodii

**HARDINESS ZONE
AND TEMPERATURE
RANGE**
9–12; 40°F–85°F

IDEAL LIGHTING
Dappled sunlight

**GROWING
LOCATION**
Outdoors/indoors

MATURE SIZE
Trails can
extend to 12'

PROPAGATION
Water or cutting
or node; spring to
early summer

Your heart will beat with joy when you see the gorgeous little heart-shaped leaves adorning this South African native. The plump leaves grow on stems that will trail and become as long as you allow them to grow. These leaves are green, with intricate marbling in silver and white, and frequently have some color on their undersides.

Special Features: Small, tubular purple flowers can emerge year-round. Once the plant flowers, it will form little nodes along the stems that are ready to root if they come in contact with soil. String of Hearts' leaves can blush deep pink or purple if you add a little direct sun to their mix.

Care Instructions: Although String of Hearts can take more water than some other succulents, they still need drainage and don't want to be left sitting in water. The pretty flowers can be encouraged with a bit of fertilizer between spring and fall. Be careful not to add too much, as the plant is susceptible to burns from too much fertilizer, which can manifest in browning and dying leaves.

Watch Out For: Yellowing leaves are an indication of too much water. Dust your plant to keep its leaves clean and fresh for optimal photosynthesis.

Arrangement Tips: Place this anywhere a spiller-style plant would be welcomed, in any kind of hanging pot. You can also set it on a shelf or a windowsill and enjoy the dangling beauty.

SILVER TORCH CACTUS

AKA WOOLY TORCH CACTUS

Cleistocactus strausii

HARDINESS ZONE AND TEMPERATURE RANGE
9-11; 20°F-85°F

IDEAL LIGHTING
Full sun to partial sun

GROWING LOCATION
Outdoors/indoors

MATURE SIZE
10' tall

PROPAGATION
Seeds, stem cuttings: summer

Silver torch is a columnar growing cactus from the mountains of Argentina and Bolivia. Like the tephrocactus and rebutia, it loves the warm heat of the summer months and the dry cool of the winter. Silver torch has a bluish-green skin with about 25 ribs on it that are covered in **areoles** (see Glossary, page 237), which, in turn, are covered in the soft silvery spines that give the plant its nickname. It is an easy-growing plant that can adapt well to life inside a home.

Special Features: Strausii takes a long time before it is ready to bloom—10 to 15 years! And once it is ready, it still needs the warmth of that summer sun and very little water in the winter for it to send out its flowers. The tubular dark-red flowers are really cool and weird, extending straight out of the side of the cactus. They don't ever fully open, but they are still attractive to hummingbirds. The blooms can cover the plant and eventually give way to a greenish fruit.

Care Instructions: Make sure to withhold most winter water, giving it a drink only every 7 to 8 weeks. Take cuttings from the offsets that branch out from the base of the plant, right above the soil.

Watch Out For: This plant attracts mealybugs, scale, and the usual indoor critters, such as aphids, spider mites, and thrips.

Arrangement Tips: Plant a silver torch cactus outside in beds where it can grow wild and spread up and out. Inside, place it in a tall, deep planter as close to a light source as possible.

PIG'S EAR

Cotyledon orbiculata

HARDINESS ZONE AND TEMPERATURE RANGE
6-11: down to 25°F

IDEAL LIGHTING
Full sun

GROWING LOCATION
Outdoors/indoors

MATURE SIZE
6-8" tall:
10-12" spread

PROPAGATION
Stem cuttings:
year-round

Cotyledon orbiculata has whitish-silvery leaves with a thin red line around their perimeters. It is a native of South Africa, where it has been used medicinally to treat warts, corns, inflammation, and even epilepsy. Its leaves are covered in a powdery dust that helps insulate the plant from extreme brightness and drought.

Special Features: From summer to fall, this shrub sends tall flower stems high above itself. Each has 10 to 20 long, asymmetrical buds that open into glorious bell-shaped flowers with silky petals turned up at the ends to show off the stamen within. This is my personal favorite of all succulent flowers.

Care Instructions: While desiring full sun, Cotyledon will tolerate partial shade. It also is a bit standoffish, generally wanting some space around itself for ventilation, which helps prevent diseases like root rot.

Watch Out For: Not many pests attack this plant, but look out for slugs and snails, and apply copper tape if the plant is in a pot that can be circled with it. Otherwise, apply pesticides.

Arrangement Tips: Pig's ear is lovely in rock gardens and in beds with aeoniums and agaves. It also makes a great feature in its own planter, where it will delight you with its warm-weather flowers.

BEAR'S PAW

Cotyledon tomentosa subsp. *Ladismithiensis*

HARDINESS ZONE AND TEMPERATURE RANGE
9–11; 25°F–80°F

IDEAL LIGHTING
Bright, filtered light

GROWING LOCATION
Outdoors/indoors

MATURE SIZE
12" tall

PROPAGATION
Leaf: year-round

Bear Paw is another fuzzy tomentosa, similar to the *Kalanchoe tomentosa* (page 134); however, the fuzzy exterior is where the similarity ends. It features yellowish-green, almost-cylindrical, curved leaves with pointy "teeth" at the top of each leaf that give it its distinctive appearance—and its nickname. The teeth can turn bright red when **stressed** (see Glossary, page 237) with sun, cold, or lack of water. In its native South Africa, Bear's Paw is known to grow in quartz fields, where the drainage is awesome.

Special Features: This plant's pretty orange-and-yellow bell-shaped blooms can begin in early spring and last most of the way through summer. In sunnier climates, flowers may arrive at surprising times in the fall and winter. Super bonus!

Care Instructions: Although it can take some more shady environments, this plant can stretch out of its usual form and get **leggy** (see Glossary, page 237) if it doesn't have enough sun. You can trim the tops for propagation and then admire your plant as it sends out new leaves and develops a bushier appearance. If you do this, make sure to put your plant in stronger light.

Watch Out For: Keep Bear's Paw dry and cool in its semi-dormant winter period. The silvery hair on the leaves can hide pests, so scan it regularly for mealybugs, scale, spider mites, and aphids.

Arrangement Tips: Bear's Paw is easy to get along with. Pair it with other cotyledons to contrast the family. You can also pair it with Tiger Jaws (page 97), Pig's Ear (page 45), or Kalanchoe 'Pink Butterflies' (page 130) for a fun, animal-themed planting. Plant with Chocolate Soldier (page 134) to create a fun fuzzy-plants arrangement.

SILVER DOLLAR JADE

Crassula arborescens

**HARDINESS ZONE
AND TEMPERATURE
RANGE**
9–11; 25°F–75°F

IDEAL LIGHTING
Full sun to
partial sun

**GROWING
LOCATION**
Outdoors/indoors;
prefers outdoors

MATURE SIZE
Can grow into a
small bush/tree
up to 4' tall and
3' wide if planted
in the ground; will
stay small in a
smaller container.

Named for the fact that its leaves are similar in size to a silver dollar, this crassula has large, thick branches that will grow easily with little or no attention once established. It has gorgeous bronze foliage with silvery-white round leaves faintly polka-dotted with red marks and a reddish stripe around the perimeter of each leaf. It is native to the Eastern and Western Capes of South Africa.

Special Features: Pretty star-shaped white flowers will emerge as this jade blooms.

Care Instructions: Plant Silver Dollar in soil that drains well. Once established, it is perfect for **xeriscape** gardens (see Glossary, page 237). It propagates very easily using stem cuttings.

Watch Out For: This plant can get quite heavy in its leaves and branches. If you want it to get tall, prune it liberally so that it doesn't hang over. Are you sure you have a Silver Dollar Jade? This plant looks quite a bit like the *Cotyledon orbiculata* (page 45). How can you be sure which you have? The flowers are completely different and will tell the tale.

Arrangement Tips: As with conventional jade, this plant will be a great specimen in a garden, pulling attention to its interesting color. Set a big rock in front of it, and plant Stone-crop Sedum (page 181) around that. The yellows and oranges of the sedum will contrast beautifully with the silvery leaves of this crassula.

RED PAGODA

Crassula capitella subsp. *thyrsiflora*

HARDINESS ZONE AND TEMPERATURE RANGE
9-11; 20°F-90°F

IDEAL LIGHTING
Full sun to partial shade

GROWING LOCATION
Outdoors/indoors

MATURE SIZE
8" tall, 18" spread

PROPAGATION
Division, offsets, leaf cutting; year-round

Native to South Africa and Namibia, this crassula has bunches of tightly packed leaves stacked on top of each other. The farther from the soil, the smaller the leaf, an arrangement that makes the plant look like a pagoda. A full pot has an awesomely geometric look. The light and bright green leaves blush at the tips and can turn a vampire red to a purplish maroon. The strange rosettes can get heavy from all of the leaves and sag over, while other rosettes push up from the center of the clump.

Special Features: Red Pagoda's tiny, star-shaped white flowers bloom in the summer on the same stem as the leaves. The foliage is both a clumper and a dangler, making it very versatile in your home garden, outside or in.

Care Instructions: Outside, shade this plant from the hottest afternoon sun. It will send runners and branch out, so choose the space you want it in and be prepared to trim it regularly if you don't want it to run wild. Inside, place it in the brightest sun available for the hottest red leaves.

Watch Out For: The standard bugs, such as mealybugs, aphids, and vine weevils, can be all over Red Pagoda. Scan your plant regularly, and use your insecticidal soap or neem oil to wipe these critters away if you see them. You can handle them, so just pay lots of attention and don't worry. You got this.

Arrangement Tips: Hang Red Pagoda in a window or plant it in a group planting with echeveria, other crassula, and Columnar Peperomia (page 153). Alternatively, plant it as a ground cover in a rock garden with tall cactus. Red Pagoda is tallish, but it gets top heavy and sags over itself, spreading out nicely into a great-looking, clumping ground cover.

WATCH CHAIN

AKA ZIPPER PLANT, RATTAIL CRASSULA

Crassula muscosa

HARDINESS ZONE AND TEMPERATURE RANGE
9–10: 30°F–70°F

IDEAL LIGHTING
Full sun to partial shade

GROWING LOCATION
Outdoors/indoors

MATURE SIZE
12" long

PROPAGATION
Cuttings: year-round

Another South African native, Watch Chain gets its nickname for the way the leaves grow in tight overlapping patterns up against each other, hiding the stem completely and looking like a living green necklace. The stems grow upright and sag gently against the weight of the leaves. Watch Chain is an easy grower and has a lifespan of about 15 years. The term *muscosa* refers to its mossy appearance. Unlike some of the other crassulas, Watch Chain has a vibrant, deep green color.

Special Features: Known for its small, star shaped yellowish-green flowers, this succulent is more likely to bloom when growing outside than inside.

Care Instructions: A small amount of fertilizer sometimes helps nudge this plant to flower. Great air circulation is helpful as well. Water it when dry, and give it the cooler morning sun, keeping it somewhat cool during the hot afternoon hours. (Placing this plant in a cool spot can help it stay sturdy if it's getting less than optimal light.) During the summer, increase the water and decrease the full sun.

Watch Out For: This plant is susceptible to mealybugs, which are treatable with alcohol. Don't overwater it, especially during the cooler months.

Arrangement Tips: Muscosa is a great container plant. Its shape and texture will provide a counterbalance to more traditional-looking succulents. It is lovely hovering over echeveria rosettes like a tree over bushes. It is also nice in **terrariums** (see Glossary, page 237), as it provides some height to balance out shorter, squatter plants.

JADE

Crassula ovata

HARDINESS ZONE AND TEMPERATURE RANGE
9–11: ideal temperature is 65°F–75°F during the day and 45°F–60°F at night

IDEAL LIGHTING
Full sun to partial sun

GROWING LOCATION
Outdoors/indoors, with as much sun as possible indoors

MATURE SIZE
Outside can grow to nearly 10' tall and spread wide and bushy, up to 6'; inside, it grows shorter and less bushy

PROPAGATION
Leaf, stem cuttings: year-round

This Native of South Africa and Mozambique is a wonderful, low-maintenance landscape plant. A firework display of flowers explodes from each clump of leaves.

Special Features: Jade has tiny, ornate flowers and leaves that are susceptible to stressing in the most beautiful way, with the leaves turning bright red as a result. This long-lasting plant makes a great gift that can endure beyond a human lifetime. It is also said to bring good luck and is one of a few with the nickname "money tree."

Care Instructions: *Crassula ovata* is very easy to care for, needing almost nothing outside and only somewhat regular bimonthly waterings inside. It doesn't want to get too dry inside and will drop leaves to let you know it is not drinking enough. You can snap off its rubbery branches and easily replant them directly into soil. Unlike many succulents, this one can be rooted in water, which makes it a nice plant to have in a bud vase in a dining room or on a coffee table.

Watch Out For: Keep an eye out for mealybugs and powdery mildew, which will look like powdered sugar. Use sulfur or a neem oil–based spray to treat the powdery mildew. You may also need to remove some of the leaves if you catch the mildew late and it is very heavy.

Arrangement Tips: This can be an ornamental ("specimen") plant in the garden, growing to tree shape and size. In cold climates it is generally grown indoors, where it will grow longer, thinner branches and spread out widely. Because of its interesting treelike shape, it can be a compelling container and terrarium plant, mimicking a bonsai tree.

CRASSULA 'CALICO KITTEN'

Crassula pellucida subsp. *marginalis* 'Variegata'

HARDINESS ZONE AND TEMPERATURE RANGE
9–11; 55°F–75°F

IDEAL LIGHTING
Full sun, partial sun, filtered sun, light shade

GROWING LOCATION
Outdoors/indoors

MATURE SIZE
2–4" tall, long trailing stems up to 12" long; will clump and spread out even farther if allowed

PROPAGATION
Root division, leaf, stem cuttings; year-round

This is a great clumping plant with stunning shades of purple, red, cream, and green on its small, stacked, heart-shaped leaves. It will spread nicely and become a gorgeous and unusual ground cover. It is native to the Eastern Cape of South Africa.

Special Features: The leaves can turn reddish-purple when stressed. This crassula will send out lovely little white firework flowers above the plant that will call attention to the brightness of its leaves.

Care Instructions: Once established, it needs very little attention; trim the flowers once they have dried. It propagates very simply with leaf and stem cuttings.

Watch Out For: Calico Kitten is prone to mealybugs and fungal issues. Keep it dry; don't overwater. Never let it sit in water, and if it is in a container with a dish, always empty the dish a few minutes after watering. The leaves are fragile, so handle as little as possible. It is sensitive to frost; keep it warm.

Arrangement Tips: This crassula clumps beautifully and looks great in hanging containers that show off its explosive white flowers blooming intermittently throughout the year. The blooms are thought to attract bees and butterflies. Drape it over shiny rocks in terrariums for an elegant look.

STRING OF BUTTONS

Crassula perforata

HARDINESS ZONE AND TEMPERATURE RANGE
9-11; 45°F-75°F

IDEAL LIGHTING
Full sun, partial sun; in very hot climates will require some afternoon shade

GROWING LOCATION
Outdoors/indoors

MATURE SIZE
1-2' tall; 2-3' wide

PROPAGATION
Leaf, stem cuttings; spring and fall

Crassulas are easy to grow and propagate and are very forgiving indoors or outside. String of Buttons, which is native to South Africa, is good in the ground, in containers, or even as a hanging plant.

Special Features: Like many crassulas, its greenish, silvery leaves are geometrically shaped and stacked on top of each other. They have pinkish edges, which will become more pronounced with full sun. The perforata sends out pretty little yellow flowers at the top that highlight the range of colors on this plant.

Care Instructions: This plant can take care of itself very well and doesn't need much water. It is also simple to propagate with offsets, stem cuttings, and leaves. Use stem cuttings high on the stalks that are less woody than the older stems below. It is very drought-tolerant and used frequently in xeriscape landscapes.

Watch Out For: There is only a low risk of pests, but watch out for mealybugs and aphids if you have it inside.

Arrangement Tips: String of Buttons will do great indoors as a companion to your haworthia or aloe. It is also nice outside among Blue Senecio (page 194) and around larger agave. It will give nice height to smaller terrarium plantings, towering over sedum and smaller echeveria.

STRING OF PEARLS

Curio rowleyanus (formerly *Senecio rowleyanus*)

HARDINESS ZONE AND TEMPERATURE RANGE
9–11; 30°F–80°F

IDEAL LIGHTING
Bright light indoors, partial shade outside

GROWING LOCATION
Outdoors/indoors

MATURE SIZE
3' trails

PROPAGATION
Cuttings; year-round

String of Pearls is a coveted succulent and a must-have for many fanatics! As the name describes, the plant is made up of stems with little pearl-shaped leaves. The stems can easily root wherever they touch soil, and when the plant is growing on the ground, it can have a walkabout and spread like ground cover.

Special Features: The blooms on the String of Pearls are notorious for their luscious whiff of spicy cinnamon. (They are one of only a few succulent flowers with a sweet odor.) Tiny daisylike blooms sprout long red stamens with bright yellow tips, then become little puffballs chock full of seeds that will spread to the wind once dry.

Care Instructions: You'll know this plant is happy when the pearls grow out lush, close together, shiny, and thick. It needs a little cool air in the winter to encourage their blooms, so make sure it is not getting too much direct light during that season. (It still needs sun, just less heat.)

Watch Out For: When it is not happy, the pearls may shrivel and dry. This is more likely to happen to young or small plants. Overwatering can result in the pearls turning brown and mushy. Regular weekly or biweekly drinks, depending on the plant's location, will be enough during most of the year. You can reduce that by half during the dormant winter. If you live where there is less light, you will want to water a little less frequently, letting the soil dry.

Arrangement Tips: This is one of the more fantastic danglers and can hold its own in any setting. Hang it inside, in a terra-cotta pot, and see how long it can grow. Outside, put it in a long, tapered planter and track its travels downward.

HARDY ICE PLANT

Delosperma cooperi

HARDINESS ZONE
AND TEMPERATURE
RANGE
6-10; in dry zones
hardy down to -20°F

IDEAL LIGHTING
Full sun

GROWING
LOCATION
Outdoors/indoors

MATURE SIZE
3-6" tall; 24" spread

PROPAGATION
Root division, stem
cuttings; spring
through fall

This noninvasive ice plant is native to southern Africa. It has fleshy little green leaves and is extremely hardy, making it a great outdoor plant in colder areas.

Special Features: Ice Plant is known for its gorgeous, daisylike magenta flowers that can carpet bloom during the warm season. The 2-inch-wide blooms make this plant a prized ornamental.

Care Instructions: It is drought-tolerant and salt-tolerant, so it can be planted near the sea. Water regularly during the first year it is planted outside, then much less to allow it to harden off to cold nights and less care. Water it a bit more when planted in containers.

Watch Out For: Ice plant must have well-draining soil and/or pots or it will grow poorly and possibly die. It is a bit prone to aphids and mealybugs; treat accordingly.

Arrangement Tips: Plant this as a spectacular ground cover on the sides of hills or in rock gardens as an accent. Fill a container for a stunning bloom and prune as needed. Plant it with sedums and sempervivums for color variety.

ECHEVERIA 'LIPSTICK'

Echeveria agavoides

HARDINESS ZONE AND TEMPERATURE RANGE
9–11; 45°F–75°F

IDEAL LIGHTING
Full sun to partial sun

GROWING LOCATION
Outdoors/indoors

MATURE SIZE
6" tall; up to 12" wide

PROPAGATION
Leaf, offset, stem cuttings; spring

This echevaria mimics the appearance of an agave, with single-spine, pointy-tipped leaves. It is easy to care for, makes lots of offsets, and gives nice flowers. It is native to Mexico, Central America, and some parts of South America.

Special Features: Lipstick has a gorgeous green color with thick, pointed leaves that get bright red on the edges (thus its name). It will get much redder depending on the amount of sun exposure; this is a great example of how a plant looks when stressed. It has pretty red flowers with yellow tips.

Care Instructions: This plant is very easy and known to flower in all four seasons once established. It does not require much care: water outside during the very hot months of summer; water bimonthly inside and let it dry in between waterings. It is frequently used in xeriscape gardens.

Watch Out For: This is a drought-tolerant plant with minimal pest issues. Look out for mealybugs and aphids; treat them with a neem oil spray.

Arrangement Tips: Lipstick is a great plant in rock gardens and around larger companion plants, including other clumping succulents. It will send out lots of offsets and create a nice family of green and red plants that will pop against dark pebbles and black lava rock. It looks great in containers with smaller plants, such as sedum, planted in a border around it.

CHROMA

Echeveria chroma

HARDINESS ZONE AND TEMPERATURE RANGE
9-11: 30°F-80°F

IDEAL LIGHTING
Full sun to partial sun

GROWING LOCATION
Outdoors/indoors

MATURE SIZE
4" rosettes

PROPAGATION
Leaf: year-round

Echeveria is a family with tons of different-colored and -shaped rosettes. Chroma is a wild variegated version, and its leaves frequently have combinations of brown, maroon, red, yellow, and creamy white. No two are the same, and they are thick and succulent. Echeveria is a true sun worshipper and thrives with a lot of bright light.

Special Features: In spring, orange-red bells with bright yellow tips and yellow coloring inside appear in clusters on Chroma's long stems. They open in turn and dry out in turn, so there are constant flowers for many weeks.

Care Instructions: Echeveria need lots of warm sun. Make sure it has great drainage wherever it is planted. If inside, make sure it is in a south-facing window, or perhaps consider a plant light to supplement the sun. Pull the flowers when they dry, and the plant will keep making new ones.

Watch Out For: Take off dead leaves, especially when growing Chroma inside, to leave no safe haven for such pests as mealybugs, gnats, and aphids. Water this plant only when dry, to protect from root rot. **Etiolation** (see Glossary, page 237) can be a problem if Chroma doesn't have enough sun; if this happens, you can cut off the rosettes and replant them if you don't like their leggy appearance.

Arrangement Tips: Outside, plant Chroma in beds with sedum, chunky rocks, aeoniums, and crassula. Inside, keep it manageable in a small pot with other echeverias. Match Chroma with Perle von Nurnberg (page 73), Blue Rose (page 69), and Lola (page 70) for awesome color combinations.

ECHEVERIA 'BLUE ROSE'

Echeveria x imbricata

HARDINESS ZONE AND TEMPERATURE RANGE
9-11; ideally 40°F-70°F; however, they can survive very brief cold spells down to about 20°F

IDEAL LIGHTING
Full sun to partial sun

GROWING LOCATION
Outdoors/indoors

MATURE SIZE
4-6" tall; 4-6" wide

PROPAGATION
Leaf and offsets; year-round

This Mexican native frequently grows **hens and chicks**–style (see Glossary, page 237). It will fill up an area nicely and clumps in tight batches.

Special Features: Blue Rose's leaves are a pretty light blue color with pinkish edges. It looks very dramatic when its orange-red flowers bloom in sequence, yielding clumps of flowers for many weeks at a time.

Care Instructions: Outside, this plant is very easy; it needs little water and a soil that drains well. Indoors you should water every two weeks and let it dry between waterings.

Watch Out For: Without enough sun, most echeveria will grow tall and leggy as they look for the light. If they get too much water, a rot could form under the soil that will kill the plant. Though they are pest-resistant, look out for mealybugs and aphids, especially if grown outside.

Arrangement Tips: Blue Rose is fantastic in rock gardens and as a companion plant to trees and larger succulents like aloe and agave. These are good container garden plants, as they will fill up a space nicely with offsets over time. As they propagate, they will press up tightly against one another, forming attractive circular patterns.

ECHEVERIA 'LOLA'

AKA HENS AND CHICKS

Echeveria 'Lola'

HARDINESS ZONE AND TEMPERATURE RANGE
9–11; 45°F–80°F

IDEAL LIGHTING
Full sun to partial shade

GROWING LOCATION
Outdoors/indoors

MATURE SIZE
4–6" tall;
6–10" spread

PROPAGATION
Leaf, offsets, stem cuttings; year-round

Like all echeveria, Lola's ancestry is traced back to Mexico. It is a hybrid of *Echeveria lilacina* and *Echeveria derenbergii*. It features small light green rosettes that grow in typical "hens and chicks" fashion, sending out babies that will form a mat of closely pressed-together plants in a planting bed. In spring and summer, it sends a short-stemmed coral-peach-yellow flower that hangs gently over the plant and is especially stunning when many bloom at once.

Special Features: Lola's coloring is remarkable. It looks like there is a pink light emanating from within the plant that sends a rosy glow just beneath the surface, giving its flesh an impressive illusion of depth.

Care Instructions: Water Lola moderately in the summer and less during the colder winter months. It loves to be outdoors in direct sun in mild-summer locations but tends to sunburn, getting ugly brown marks on its leaves in temperatures over 80°F. Unlike some succulents, whose papery dead bottom leaves provide protection for the rosette from water and decay, this plant's dead leaves can serve as a nest for pests, so remove them immediately.

Watch Out For: Moths and caterpillars might chew holes in the leaves. Look for them on the underside of the leaves and discard them and their eggs. Treat the plant with a neem oil–based spray. Make sure your plant gets at least three to five hours of sun if it is living inside. Echeveria is prone to getting leggy without enough light: its rosettes rise up high from the soil, searching for the sun. If the appearance bothers you, trim the head of the rosette, and after it calluses over, replant it in fresh succulent soil.

Arrangement Tips: Plant this succulent in beds, where it will have room to spread and fill in with offsets. It is great in container gardens with sedum and portulacaria and lovely as a stand-alone plant in a decorative pot.

PERLE VON NURNBERG

Echeveria 'Perle von Nurnberg'

HARDINESS ZONE AND TEMPERATURE RANGE
9-10, 30°F-75°F

IDEAL LIGHTING
Full sun to partial sun

GROWING LOCATION
Outdoors/indoors

MATURE SIZE
6-8" tall

PROPAGATION
Leaf: year-round

Native to Mexico, Perle von Nurnberg is a popular cultivar and the love child of *Echeveria elegans* and *Echeveria gibbiflora*. It is grayish-purple and will brighten significantly when exposed to bright sun. Perle von Nurnberg's vibrancy and beauty will make it the focus of any garden or planter you put it in. It is also known for the **epicuticular wax**, or **farina** (see Glossary, page 237), that looks like a powdery coating on its leaves. This powder covers the entire leaf and helps protect internal water from evaporating as well as provides a natural protection again sunburn. Touch the plant as little as possible to avoid rubbing off this wax.

Special Features: Like many echeverias, this succulent sends out a jumbly stem with many coral pink flowers along it. It can bloom many times a year if it is given sufficient light and water.

Care Instructions: Make sure this plant is exposed to 3 to 4 hours of bright light a day, preferably the gentler morning sun. The brighter the light, the prettier the colors that will emerge on the leaves; they sometimes even get frosty pink tips along the edges. Beheading is a great way to save any plants that have etiolated. You can replant the top piece, which will reroot and begin to grow again.

Watch Out For: Overwatering can be disastrous for this echeveria, which will shrink into itself and disintegrate in the wrong conditions. Most echeveria will go into a state of etiolation (typically called "getting leggy") if they don't get enough sun. When this happens, the stem grows toward the light source, leaving the rosette higher off the soil. If this happens, consider propagation by beheading.

Arrangement Tips: Pair this plant with other bright-colored succulents in a pot with great drainage. Balance the purple with yellow Coppertone Stonecrop sedum (page 181) and Black Prince echeverias. Use a spiller plant such as String of Pearls (page 61) to flesh out your creation.

MEXICAN FIRECRACKER

AKA FIRECRACKER PLANT, HENS AND CHICKS

Echeveria setosa

HARDINESS ZONE AND TEMPERATURE RANGE
9-11: 30°F-80°F

IDEAL LIGHTING
Full sun to partial sun

GROWING LOCATION
Outdoors/indoors

MATURE SIZE
3-5" tall: 24" spread

PROPAGATION
Leaf: year-round

An explosion of bright red flowers with yellow tips gives this unusual echeveria its nickname. The flowers can start in early spring and come in waves through fall. Native to Mexico, like all echeveria, setosa is a slow grower that may not get to full size for five years.

Special Features: This is one of an interesting subset of succulents that are covered in thick, short white hairs. It is said that the hairs of this fuzzy plant provide various protections for the plant, including insulation. Setosa is more cold-hardy than some other succulents, which may prove that theory.

Care Instructions: Though it is drought-tolerant, setosa actually likes regular water during the summer growth months. Water weekly, but don't let it sit in wet soil or a full water dish. During the winter dormant months, barely water at all.

Watch Out For: It is prone to mealybugs, vine weevil, and aphids. These bugs will kill your plant eventually if left alone, so check it regularly and treat accordingly.

Arrangement Tips: When in bloom, setosa will look great wherever it is: rock gardens, container gardens, or even hanging gardens. Pair it with other fuzzy plants, like *Kalanchoe tomentosa* (page 134), for an interesting juxtaposition, or with semps, sedums, and delosperma for a floral feast for the eyes.

GOLDEN BARREL
AKA MOTHER-IN-LAW'S CUSHION
Echinocactus grusonii 'Golden Barrel'

**HARDINESS ZONE
AND TEMPERATURE
RANGE**
9–12, 45°F–80°F

IDEAL LIGHTING
Full sun to
partial sun

**GROWING
LOCATION**
Outdoors/indoors

MATURE SIZE
2' tall; 3' spread

PROPAGATION
Seed; spring
to summer

Golden Barrel is a favorite of many cactus collectors. It is a spherical plant and grows quickly initially, then slows dramatically. It might take 10 years to reach 10 inches in diameter, but it will continue to grow, and eventually a mature specimen can be 3 feet wide (outside, they tend to grow faster). Over time, the shape can elongate so that it more closely resembles a barrel. The light green, ribbed sphere is covered in yellowish spines that run down the edges of the ribs, and there is a large patch of fuzz on the top of the plant.

Special Features: Golden Barrel can produce 2- to 3-inch yellow flowers in a crown formation around the top of the circle, but usually not until the plant is 10 to 20 years old. The flowers are diurnal, meaning they open during the day and close at night.

Care Instructions: Place your Golden Barrel in a sunny spot, but protect it from the harshest sun, which can burn its skin. Water in the morning or at night to avoid creating sunburn spots.

Watch Out For: Golden Barrel is mostly critter-free but can be susceptible to scale and mealybugs. As with all succulents, don't overwater as the plant can develop bacterial and fungal infections from sitting in wet soil.

Arrangement Tips: Add some sedum to the soil floor around your golden barrel, or even a dangling plant like String of Hearts (page 41). Place two in tall planters on either side of your gate or the entrance to your home. Place it in a dark planter on a pedestal in the window to give it the regal treatment it deserves.

RAINBOW HEDGEHOG

AKA RUBY RAINBOW CACTUS

Echinocereus rigidissimus rubrispinus

HARDINESS ZONE AND TEMPERATURE RANGE
9–11, 20°F–90°F

IDEAL LIGHTING
Full sun to partial sun

GROWING LOCATION
Outdoors/indoors

MATURE SIZE
10" tall

PROPAGATION
Seed: early fall

This glorious, slow-growing cactus is a Mexican native. Beloved for its red and pink coloring, it is one of the most sought-after plants in the cactus world. Its radial spines, which cover the surface of the plant, emerge deep red and magenta, then fade to a pinkish yellow over time. This frequently gives the plant an interesting bicolor appearance, with a lighter pink base at the bottom and a brighter, reddish look at the top.

Special Features: The Rainbow Hedgehog also produces large magenta flowers that are just as magical as the spines. (Not all beautiful plants *also* have beautiful flowers—but this one does.) After a few months, the flower gives way to a dark purple fruit, from which seeds can be harvested for propagation.

Care Instructions: Water delicately in the spring and summer, and withhold water significantly in the dormant winter. It should be dry and cool in the winter. Keeping it in a cool habitat during these months will cause it to shrink on a cellular level, further decreasing its need for water.

Watch Out For: Root rot can be a problem for Rainbow Hedgehog, as it has a shallow, weak root system. This is only a problem if your plant is sitting in wet soil, so just pay good attention and it should be fine. Add some extra **pumice** (see Glossary, page 237) to your soil, which will help with drainage.

Arrangement Tips: Rainbow Hedgehog is so showy, it almost begs to be alone in a pot where it can hear you recite sweet, loving poems to its beauty without wondering who else you might be talking to.

PEANUT CACTUS

Echinopsis chamaecereus 'Peanut Cactus'

HARDINESS ZONE AND TEMPERATURE RANGE
10–11, 40°F–90°F

IDEAL LIGHTING
Inside, bright direct sun; outside, direct sun with some protection from afternoon rays

GROWING LOCATION
Outdoors/indoors

MATURE SIZE
6" tall, 1–2" wide per stem

PROPAGATION
Stem cuttings: in the fall, after plant is done flowering

The Peanut Cactus, an Argentinian native, has lots of thin, ribbed stems covered with soft yet skin-piercing spines. It grows in all different directions, matting and clumping with abandon. It loves the sun, so give it as much as possible, especially indoors. It wants some light protection from the heat of the afternoon sun.

Special Features: The flowers are spectacular batches of red-orange funnels that can arrive with numerous buds. They are diurnal (open during the day, closed at night) and last only about a week.

Care Instructions: During the winter dormancy, if it is cool enough (40°F to 50°F), Peanut Cactus won't need any water. A little dryness in appearance is normal during this time and will encourage those amazing spring blooms. During summer, water it thoroughly when the soil is dry a few inches down.

Watch Out For: Any sudden change in temperature or movement can cause the buds to drop before they open. Because it doesn't like humidity, this is not a great bathroom plant. Spider mites and mealybugs have been known to attack this plant. Use gloves and spray and wipe off these critters if you get an outbreak.

Arrangement Tips: This is a great hanging plant once it is established. It also looks great in a dish with other small cacti.

DOMINO CACTUS

AKA EASTER LILY CACTUS, NIGHT-BLOOMING HEDGEHOG

Echinopsis subdenudata or *Echinopsis ancistrophora*

HARDINESS ZONE AND TEMPERATURE RANGE
9-11; 25°F-85°F

IDEAL LIGHTING
Full sun to partial shade

GROWING LOCATION
Outdoors/indoors

MATURE SIZE
Generally 4" tall (but can elongate up to 12"); 4-5" wide

PROPAGATION
Offsets; spring to summer after plant is done flowering

This South American native, from the hills and mountains of Bolivia and Paraguay, is mostly spineless and easy to handle; it is also notable for the numerous white dots along its 8 to 12 ribs. Its hardy nature and modern look, combined with its extraordinary large and fragrant flowers, make it an excellent cactus companion for your home.

Special Features: Domino Cactus has tall, stemmed flowers that can sit 5" to 9" off the surface of the plant. The stems emerge from the areoles near the top of the round cactus. Areoles can be where a cactus produces spines, but in this plant, it is just full of fuzzy white hairs toward the top. Domino Cactus has special blooms, which last all night the day they first open but then begin to decay quickly and are completely done by the end of the following day. They have a delicate fragrance and an elegant beauty.

Care Instructions: Keep this cactus in a bright spot, as it needs sun. Water it every two weeks or so, but make sure it is dry before watering to avoid root rot.

Watch Out For: Domino Cactus is susceptible to mites and aphids, and its color fades to yellow or orange if it gets too much direct sun. This plant can deal with higher humidity than many cacti (30 percent), so it could potentially live in a well-ventilated bathroom. It is also a winter dormant plant, so water it much less and keep it in a cool environment during those months.

Arrangement Tips: Keep this with other cacti in a mixed pot, as they have similar watering needs. Alone in a pot, it will be remarkable during its flowering season.

FISHBONE CACTUS

AKA ZIGZAG CACTUS, QUEEN OF THE NIGHT

Epiphyllum anguliger or *Disocactus anguliger*

HARDINESS ZONE AND TEMPERATURE RANGE
10–11; 35°F–75°F

IDEAL LIGHTING
Bright filtered light

GROWING LOCATION
Outdoors/indoors

MATURE SIZE
12" leaves with a wide spread

PROPAGATION
Division or stem cuttings; year-round

Fishbone cactus gets its name from its foliage. Each stem is flat, and the leaves have wide lobes that make it look like a fish skeleton. It will branch heavily, and the main stem may get woody over time while the rest stay green and floppy. This is an **epiphytic** plant (see Glossary, page 237), meaning that in its native Mexican environment it likes to attach itself to other plants.

Special Features: Fishbone is an **epiphyllum** (see Glossary, page 237), which are mostly night bloomers. Its long, showy buds open to yellow or white flowers with gorgeous pointy petals and a deeply sweet, intoxicating fragrance. Pay attention when the buds start to form; the flower's life is brief, and it will start to die off by the following morning.

Care Instructions: Fishbone likes filtered light. Too much sun and it can get burned. Give a bit more light to get it to flower. It likes humidity, especially in fall and winter, so feel free to mist daily during those seasons. It may not bloom until it is four to six years old. As with many plants that don't always bloom indoors, you can feed Fishbone a half-strength fertilizer during its grow seasons; that may put it over the top.

Watch Out For: This plant's small, hard-to-notice spines can hurt, so use caution when handling it. Sunburn will manifest as an orange or red patch on the skin. Keep an eye out for mealybugs and aphids, too.

Arrangement Tips: Fishbone is a great hanging plant with long leaves that dangle down. You can give it a moss pole or trellis and train it to climb all over them. Its foliage is the main attraction, so make sure it has room to be fully admired. It can be awesome in a stand-alone pot, outside or by a bright window.

QUEEN OF THE NIGHT

AKA DUTCHMAN'S PIPE CACTUS, NIGHT-BLOOMING CEREUS

Epiphyllum oxypetalum

HARDINESS ZONE AND TEMPERATURE RANGE
10-11: down to 50°F

IDEAL LIGHTING
Bright filtered light

GROWING LOCATION
Outdoors/indoors

MATURE SIZE
8'-10' tall

PROPAGATION
Leaf, stem cuttings: year-round

Not actually in the Cereus family, this Central American native has its nickname because it generally blooms only at night, and each bloom lasts for only one or two nights. The long, notched, waxy leaves are on flattened stems that won't grow upward without support. Because the foliage is bright green and propagates very easily, you will sometimes see vendors selling individual leaves with the name and flower type written in marker on the leaf.

Special Features: The flower buds grow very long, 7 to 10 inches, and will finally open just briefly in the middle of the night. The fragrance is intoxicating, especially if a batch of buds all open at once. It can have many crops of flowers over the course of one season. The buds are pink, and the flowers are a silky white.

Care Instructions: This plant wants moderate water, only when dry. During summer it likes a bit of humidity. Cold weather during the drier winter months will encourage summer blooms.

Watch Out For: Mealybugs, aphids, and spider mites might try to make a home in your plant. It is also prone to root rot, especially in the winter. Water it sparingly during those months.

Arrangement Tips: Queen of the Night is great in a hanging basket. It will also grow upward with stakes and can be trained to grow up and around windows. Plant it with a flowering cactus for a nice juxtaposition.

GHOST EUPHORBIA

AKA AFRICAN CANDELABRA, THE PALE EUPHORBIA

Euphorbia ammak 'Variegata'

HARDINESS ZONE AND TEMPERATURE RANGE
9–11; down to 35°F

IDEAL LIGHTING
Full sun to partial shade

GROWING LOCATION
Outdoors/indoors

MATURE SIZE
15–30' tall; 6–12' wide

PROPAGATION
Stem cuttings: spring and summer

African Candelabra is actually not found on continental Africa but on the Arabian Peninsula, specifically in Saudi Arabia and Yemen. The variegated version of the euphorbia grows tall and spreads its branches to resemble a giant candelabra.

Special Features: Ghost Euphorbia features marbling variegated patterns in its yellow-whitish flesh, with reddish-brown edging and spines. The yellow-green flowers that emerge on top in spring will give way to an inedible greenish fruit.

Care Instructions: This slow grower wants some shade in very hot climates and will grow a little faster with regular summer water. It should get dry between waterings to avoid root rot. This succulent does not love the wind, so plant it in a protected location. You can prune it for shape and form. Don't forget to propagate the cuttings, which should re-root in soil after being allowed to dry and scab over.

Watch Out For: Most euphorbias feature an irritating milky sap that can damage your eyes, so use gloves and eye gear when handling and pruning this plant. Ghost Euphorbia has been known to topple over with too much water, wind, or a combination of both.

Arrangement Tips: Grow it in a container inside in a bright, sunny corner. Outdoors, grow it as a focal point in a sunny spot protected from the wind.

BASEBALL PLANT
AKA SEA URCHIN CACTUS
Euphorbia obesa

HARDINESS ZONE AND TEMPERATURE RANGE
10-11; 30°F-100°F

IDEAL LIGHTING
Full sun to partial shade

GROWING LOCATION
Outdoors/indoors

MATURE SIZE
8" tall

PROPAGATION
Stem cuttings of offsets; year-round

The euphorbia family is a fascinating one, consisting of an enormous variety of cactus-like plants and shrubs, both small and large. Baseball plant is one of the most fabulous specimens. Its early life is characterized by its round stem, which has tiny bumps up the sides that resemble the stitching on a baseball (hence its common name). It is a green plant when grown in shade and can get a purplish blush when exposed to strong sun. As it grows, it can elongate and form a bloated cylinder that retains a lot of personality.

Special Features: Obesa is a **dioecious** plant (see Glossary, page 237), meaning that each individual specimen has either male or female flowers. You can tell which you have by paying close attention to the **cyathia** (see Glossary, page 237), the little growth from which the flowers emerge. The male will send out a batch of up to five flowers, but the female plant will develop only one. The flowers require cross pollination to develop into fruit, which will bear seeds.

Care Instructions: Baseball plant is quite simple to care for. Be careful not to overwater it; in its natural habitat in South Africa, it might get only 12 inches of rainfall a year. Water infrequently but thoroughly, and don't let it sit in wet soil or a full dish. Expose it to great light, but don't worry if it gets some shade.

Watch Out For: This euphorbia is generally pest-free, but look out for the usual indoor bugs.

Arrangement Tips: Obesa is such a charming and unusual plant that will look remarkable in its own little pot in a window or near a plant light source inside. Outside, plant this succulent under trees and other shrubs where it is sure to get solid filtered light.

STICKS ON FIRE

AKA FIRE STICKS, RED PENCIL TREE, MILKBUSH

Euphorbia tirucalli 'Sticks on Fire'

HARDINESS ZONE AND TEMPERATURE RANGE
10–12; 30°F–100°F

IDEAL LIGHTING
Full sun

GROWING LOCATION
Outdoors/indoors (but will get a lot bigger outside)

MATURE SIZE
8' tall

PROPAGATION
Cuttings; year-round

Sticks on Fire is a segmented euphorbia that grows long, pencil-thin erect branches that are filled with white milky sap that is very toxic to the skin. This version of the tirucalli produces gorgeous bright red and pink foliage that can fade to yellow or green when receiving less daily sun. It is a native to Madagascar and parts of southern Africa.

Special Features: Sticks on Fire's most remarkable feature is the brightness of its branches, which look vibrant and electric when sun is shining through them. Keep this plant in as much sun as possible and it will command attention and receive compliments.

Care Instructions: For a plant like Sticks on Fire, it is imperative that you expose it to as much sun as possible if you grow it indoors (at least 5 to 6 hours). South-facing windows will generally get you the most light. A plant grow light might also really improve its ability to thrive inside. Water minimally during the summer (every one to two weeks), and even less during the winter (three to four weeks); adjust for spells of extra hot weather with more water during those periods. Use protective gloves when handling euphorbias and beware the sap; it is toxic.

Watch Out For: Sunburn can be an issue for this plant if the weather gets very hot suddenly. When it needs more water, its leaves will look limp and shriveled.

Arrangement Tips: Plant Sticks on Fire outside in beds, as borders and barriers, or just as a specimen plant to the side of your front door, greeting you in all its glory when you arrive home. Keep it far enough to the side where stray hands won't grab at it, potentially exposing its toxic milk. Inside, plant it in tall planters by windows where it can settle in for the long haul.

AFRICAN MILK TREE

Euphorbia trigona 'Rubra'

HARDINESS ZONE AND TEMPERATURE RANGE
10–11; 50°F–90°F

IDEAL LIGHTING
Bright light

GROWING LOCATION
Outdoors/indoors

MATURE SIZE
9' (outside), 6' (inside), with a candelabra spread

PROPAGATION
Cutting: spring and summer

Euphorbia trigona 'Rubra' is a pretty red-and-green plant from central Africa. Its stem is three-sided with paired spines along the edges and short-lived leaves that grow on the edges with the spines. It can produce small white-and-yellow flowers but blooms almost exclusively when grown outside and only once fully mature.

Special Features: Trigona has gorgeous, mottled green and light green skin, and the name *'Rubra'* indicates a varietal with skin that blushes reddish to maroon. It is a simple and elegant plant that can be remarkable as a little window plant and a downright statement plant once it gets some size.

Care Instructions: Give this plant nice bright light and moderate warmth, and it will reward you by being attractive and not very needy. It doesn't like cold or frost. When propagating, let the cuttings dry before putting them back in new soil. Wait 7 to 10 days to water. Use gloves when handling and beware the sap; it is toxic.

Watch Out For: Like most succulents, African Milk Tree wants to dry out between waterings and can rot if it is sitting in wet soil. However, it may want weekly water during the growing summer months and can also have problems if it is left without water for too long. It doesn't like humidity, so keep it somewhere dry. This is not a good bathroom plant.

Arrangement Tips: The color begs to be paired with other bright plants, such as Coppertone Stonecrop sedum (page 181) and Perle von Nurnberg echeveria (page 73). It also looks fantastic in a pot by itself, standing tall and alone.

TIGER JAWS

Faucaria tigrina

HARDINESS ZONE AND TEMPERATURE RANGE
9–11; 25°F–90°F

IDEAL LIGHTING
Full sun to partial sun

GROWING LOCATION
Outdoors/indoors

MATURE SIZE
5" tall; clumping to 12"

PROPAGATION
Offsets; year-round

This is a very toothy plant! Its green triangular leaves have little downward-facing spines along the edges that look curiously like teeth. Leaves open opposite each other, making what looks like a pair of jaws. (The plant actually uses these teeth to trap moisture from the air.) The leaves form rosettes, and the rosettes clump, which opens the possibility of many flowering at once. Plant them together in one pot.

Special Features: Statuesque, thick buds emerge from the center of the rosettes in fall and through winter, and these buds give way to large, bright yellow, daisylike flowers with tons of thin, little petals. The blooms open on sunny days for a few afternoon hours.

Care Instructions: If your plant is a baby, it may not bloom for a few years while it gives its energy to growth. It also needs a good 3 to 4 hours of solid daily sun in order to flower. Even more solid sun will cause the leaves to turn colors, from reds to purples. Sometimes just the teeth will blush.

Watch Out For: Overwatering proves tragic for the faucaria family; the plants' flesh melts into an almost-gelatinous mess when they absorb too much fluid. Keep Tiger Jaws dry, and resist watering until you are sure the soil is completely dry. Mealybugs have been known to like this plant, so keep an eye out.

Arrangement Tips: I usually keep this one by itself in a window or table planter in a very bright room. It is fun to look at any time of the year, and when the bloom comes, it offers very nice company.

LITTLE WARTY

Gasteria batesiana x Gasteria 'Old Man Silver'

HARDINESS ZONE AND TEMPERATURE RANGE
9–11: down to 25°F

IDEAL LIGHTING
Full sun to partial shade

GROWING LOCATION
Outdoors/indoors

MATURE SIZE
6-8" tall; 6-8" wide

PROPAGATION
Offsets, leaf; spring and summer

A gasteria native to South Africa, this plant is similar to a haworthia and will grow in the same conditions. It is a great indoor succulent as long as it receives bright light and moderate water during its active months, in the spring and summer.

Special Features: Larger than the dwarf bicolor, Little Warty has very thick, almost-plastic-feeling stemless leaves featuring swirls of dark and light green with creamy mottling in the center.

Care Instructions: Drought-tolerant, this plant likes to be left fairly dry during the winter months and a bit moist during the summer and spring. It is known to flourish with monthly liquid fertilizer feedings during those growth months. In spring, when it fills its pot, repot it in a slightly larger but still shallow vessel.

Watch Out For: Gasterias are susceptible to fungus and mealybugs, so water sparingly, keeping the moisture in the soil and not on the plant. Track and treat any bugs on the plant.

Arrangement Tips: Contrast Little Warty with Dasyphyllum (page 174) or Cape Blanco sedum (page 185). Outside, plant it under taller succulents like aeoniums or aloes. Plant it alone in small planters that will match the scale of the plant, and make sure your planter has drainage.

OX TONGUE

AKA DWARF TONGUE

Gasteria bicolor var. liliputana

HARDINESS ZONE AND TEMPERATURE RANGE
9-11; down to 25°F

IDEAL LIGHTING
Partial shade to full sun

GROWING LOCATION
Outdoors/indoors

MATURE SIZE
3-5" tall;
4-6" spread

PROPAGATION
Offsets, leaf;
year-round

Native to the Eastern Cape of South Africa, this gasteria grows well indoors with bright light and moderate water in the spring and summer.

Special Features: Its thick, fleshy reptilian leaves—dark green and mottled with creamy markings—are shaped like tongues. Liliputana is the dwarf version of this plant; other versions can get quite a bit larger. In midwinter to spring, it makes pretty flowers that are reddish pink and full of nectar. The plant is long-stemmed and can send blooms up to 5 feet away from their tiny parent.

Care Instructions: Drought-tolerant, this plant likes to be left fairly dry during the winter months and a bit moist during the spring and summer. It is known to flourish with monthly liquid fertilizer feedings during those growth months. In spring, when it fills its pot, repot it in a slightly larger but still shallow vessel.

Watch Out For: Ox Tongue can get fungal infections from too much water or even from water on its leaves. This will manifest as black spots on the leaves. The plant can fight back and recover from this if the conditions that caused it are altered. Generally, this means less humidity and more careful waterings. It can also be susceptible to mealybugs, so treat accordingly.

Arrangement Tips: Grow this succulent indoors in shallow planters and outdoors under taller plants that will provide shade. It will turn reddish when stressed, so give it a small amount of direct sun if you can.

LAVENDER PEBBLES

AKA JEWEL LEAF PLANT, MOON ROCKS

Graptopetalum amethystinum

HARDINESS ZONE AND TEMPERATURE RANGE
9-11; 35°F-85°F

IDEAL LIGHTING
Full sun to partial sun; likes some shade

GROWING LOCATION
Outdoors/indoors

MATURE SIZE
4-6" tall; 12-18" spread

PROPAGATION
Leaf, offsets; year-round

The name Lavender Pebbles is quite accurate for this plant, as the leaves are plump and round and have a pink-violet-purple-and-silver coloring. This Mexican native also has an interesting powdery coating on its leaves. It looks quite arresting when many plants grow together in a large clump, making it difficult to tell which leaf belongs to which rosette.

Special Features: Its spring blooms are star-shaped and yellow, with red triangles on the tips. The blooming may continue through summer and into fall.

Care Instructions: Lavender Pebbles is great outdoors in well-draining soil. In very hot regions, it will require afternoon shade. Water moderately during the spring and summer, but keep the soil mostly dry during the cold months.

Watch Out For: This plant doesn't love the frost, as the leaves are so fat and full of water. Cover it with frost cloth if it is outside during a surprise cold spell. It is not known to be particularly attractive to pests, but always keep an eye out for mealybugs and aphids.

Arrangement Tips: The fantastic colors on this plant will complement many other bright succulents, such as aeoniums like Zwartkop (page 6) and Sunburst (page 13). Keep it in a container inside so you can more closely admire it. Use it in a hanging basket; the spill can get to 18 inches long. It's also pretty in planting beds with chunky rocks.

FRED IVES

x Graptoveria 'Fred Ives'

HARDINESS ZONE AND TEMPERATURE RANGE
9–11; 20°–70°F

IDEAL LIGHTING
Full Sun

GROWING LOCATION
Outdoors/indoors (only with fantastic light)

MATURE SIZE
2' tall

PROPAGATION
Leaf/cuttings: year-round

Fred Ives—a combination of *Graptopetalum paraguayense* and *Echeveria gibbiflora*—is a real crowd pleaser with a variety of colors that blush across its surface. Depending on the light it gets, Fred Ives can be any combination of blue, gray, purple, orange, yellow, and salmon, sometimes all right on the same leaf! It is a thick-stalked plant that branches and sends out pretty rosettes. The stems can be 3 to 4 inches thick when mature. This plant loves the sun, so if you grow it inside, make sure it gets 3 to 4 bright hours at a minimum.

Special Features: This succulent sends out long, jumbled flower stems that can be 2 inches long and are bursting with small, star-shaped, white-yellow-and-orange flowers. Flowering mostly occurs during summer, but in sunnier locations, it can keep going deep into autumn.

Care Instructions: When Fred Ives is planted inside, it is very important to keep it out of wet soil situations, so make sure to have great drainage. It is less forgiving than some other succulents and can form root rot rather quickly. Don't touch the leaves with your fingers, if possible.

Watch Out For: Watch out for mealybugs, aphids, and other pests in humid locations. Give it plenty of air circulation.

Arrangement Tips: Outside, plant Fred Ives in rock gardens and under trees, along paths, and near larger plants. Inside, plant it alone in a large planter, and keep it near your brightest windows.

GHOST PLANT

Graptopetalum paraguayense

HARDINESS ZONE AND TEMPERATURE RANGE
9–11; 20°F–85°F

IDEAL LIGHTING
Full sun to partial shade

GROWING LOCATION
Outdoors/indoors

MATURE SIZE
12" tall

PROPAGATION
Stem or leaf cuttings: spring or summer
Offsets: spring

The Ghost Plant, native to Mexico, is another color shifter; it can even change colors as the seasons progress. When growing in brighter and warmer sun, it develops yellows and oranges, while in the cooler months, it shifts to grays, blues, and purples. Ghost Plant has a flattish, roughly 4-inch rosette with stems that can get thick as the plant matures. Although this is mostly an upright plant, when the rosettes get leggy, the stems may bend over and cause it to become a trailing plant with dangling rosettes, which can look fantastic.

Special Features: Ghost Plant produces star-shaped flowers similar to Fred Ives but on shorter stems, and it will bloom from early spring through summer.

Care Instructions: Water mildly inside and only when dry. Outside, there may be very little care at all. When happy, paraguayense will send out tons of offsets that will fill up a nice area around the mother plant.

Watch Out For: Keep an eye out for mealybugs, vine weevils, and aphids. Shriveled leaves will let you know if you haven't watered enough; the plant will bounce back soon after it gets enough moisture.

Arrangement Tips: Ghost Plant is great in most settings. Outside, it looks awesome in a rock garden or next to blue, chalky senecio plants and Coppertone Stonecrop sedum (page 181). It will also highlight other bright, colorful succulents. Ghost Plant can also look great on its own, trailing in a hanging planter.

OPALINA

Graptoveria 'Opalina'

This plant reminds me of the coloring of Echeveria 'Lola', but with thicker, wider, and rounder leaves. It has whitish, blushing swirls of blues, greens, and purples in its leaves, which get pinker toward the edges and are more pronounced with bright direct sun. It was named for its similarity to the shifting colors of an opal. This plant is a hybrid of *Echeveria colorata* and *Graptopetalum amethystinum*. Its parents are native to Mexico and the United States, and it was created in California.

 Special Features: Pretty blooms of yellow and orange will erupt on short stems in spring and summer.

 Care Instructions: Water this plant moderately, and never when the soil is still wet. The plant can grow leggy and tumble over a planter lip. Its stems will send out roots and connect itself to the soil as it moves along in nature. In a pot, it may become a hanging plant as it becomes top-heavy. You can leave it as is or cut off the rosettes and repot them once the stems callous.

Watch Out For: Root rot is a concern, so be careful when watering, especially during the winter months.

Arrangement Tips: Plant Opalina with tall branches of portulacaria above it, or next to green-and-blue echeverias. Plant it with big pebbles in containers and in beds. Place it where it will get a few hours of sun but some shade, too, to prevent sunburn.

DANCING BONES CACTUS

AKA DRUNKARD'S DREAM, SPICE CACTUS, BOTTLE CACTUS

Hatiora salicornioides or *Rhipsalis salicornioides*

HARDINESS ZONE AND TEMPERATURE RANGE
10-12: down to 25°F-30°F

IDEAL LIGHTING
Light shade to full sun

GROWING LOCATION
Outdoors/indoors

MATURE SIZE
12-18" tall: 12-18" spread

PROPAGATION
Stem cuttings, root vision: spring

Small and bushy, Dancing Bones Cactus is native to Brazil, where it grows epiphytically in dappled sunlight below the canopy of the rain forest. It is mostly spineless, but an older plant may develop spiny growth around its base. It is made up of little sections of bottle- or sausage-shaped foliage connected to each other in segments.

Special Features: Its small, bell-shaped flowers of deep orange and yellow pop out of slender branches and eventually give way to translucent reddish berries.

Care Instructions: Give Dancing Bones indirect bright light, and feed it regularly with water and fertilizer during its spring and summer growing months. Water only occasionally, and do not fertilize it during its winter dormancy. Propagate it simply by breaking off the little branches and replanting them in soil.

Watch Out For: Very few pests will hurt this plant; avoid direct sun and overwatering.

Arrangement Tips: Because this plant is humidity tolerant, it is an excellent choice for terrariums with cactus, gasteria, and sedum. Will also look great in hanging baskets and container gardens. It can be pruned for shape.

COOPER'S HAWORTHIA

AKA PUSSY FOOT, WINDOW HAWORTHIA

Haworthia cooperi var. obtusa

HARDINESS ZONE AND TEMPERATURE RANGE
9-12: 50°F-90°F

IDEAL LIGHTING
Partial shade, bright indirect light

GROWING LOCATION
Shady outdoors in warm climates/indoors

MATURE SIZE
1-3" tall; 4-6" spread with pups

PROPAGATION
Offsets, leaf; year-round

Cooper's is native to South Africa's Eastern Cape. Many varietals of cooperi have a buried stem and gelatinous, translucent, and veiny leaves that just reach the surface of the soil. These leaves are sometimes referred to as "windows" because you can see through them deep into the plant. The windows allow light to reach the photosynthetic cells, which, unlike in most plants, are buried deep within the leaf.

Special Features: This plant will flower similarly to *Haworthia fasciata* (page 114). In different varietals, the leaves will display many colors in the windows, from oranges to reds, yellows, and purples.

Care Instructions: Propagate your haworthia by removing pups. Water it infrequently while it develops new roots. It needs a minimal amount of fertilizer in the spring and fall to strengthen it for the growing season and prop it up during the dormant winter. Water it only when dry; the plant is prone to root rot.

Watch Out For: It's a slow grower, so don't expect this plant to look very different for the first year or two.

Arrangement Tips: Pick a pot that matches (or contrasts with) your Cooper's color. Make sure to place it near a window where you will be able to watch the sun shine through it.

ZEBRA PLANT

Haworthia fasciata or Haworthiopsis fasciata

HARDINESS ZONE AND TEMPERATURE RANGE
9-11: 50°F–80°F

IDEAL LIGHTING
Partial shade, bright indirect light

GROWING LOCATION
Shady outdoors/indoors

MATURE SIZE
3-5" tall:
7-8" spread

PROPAGATION
Offsets, leaf:
year-round

Zebra Plant has thick, triangular leaves that grow in tight upturned rosettes with dotted white stripes like drips of frosting. It is native to South Africa's Eastern Cape.

Special Features: The plant will send a dainty white (sometimes pinkish) flower with thin brown stripes far away from itself, like a kite on a string. The stem can be up to 16 inches long! When stressed, the leaves will turn very red, giving it an exotic look. It will turn green again with less extreme heat.

Care Instructions: Water infrequently as the Zebra Plant develops new roots. You can fertilize it monthly during the April-to-September growing season if your plant is languishing or you haven't repotted and the soil is very dry and crumbly. Don't fertilize it during the dormant winter. Water it only when dry; it is prone to root rot. Propagate your Zebra Plant by removing pups.

Watch Out For: Your plant will close up like a spider to conserve its energy if it is thirsty. Black spots forming on the leaves are a sign of overwatering. Common bugs to keep an eye out for are mealybugs and spider mites.

Arrangement Tips: This will look great in a small planter that matches the petite stature of the plant. It looks great in just about anything, but pay attention to the coloring of the dish: It will look modern and sculptural in a black pot, wild and natural in terra-cotta, and clean and organized in white.

STAR CACTUS

Haworthia retusa

HARDINESS ZONE AND TEMPERATURE RANGE
9–11, 45°F–90°F

IDEAL LIGHTING
Partial sun to partial shade

GROWING LOCATION
Outdoors/indoors

MATURE SIZE
5" tall

PROPAGATION
Offsets; year-round

Retusa is a window succulent like the cooperi. This term refers to the "windows" on the edges of the plant's very shiny leaves, which allow light to get deep inside where the photosynthesis cells live. Star Cactus frequently grows with much of the plant underground and just the window leaves open to the sun. It gets its name from the fact that the leaves curve downward at the end. It can range in color from a bright rich green to almost brown in the wild, depending on how much sun it gets.

Special Features: The Star Cactus produces small, tubular flowers that extend from a tall floral stem, which can be even longer than some of the other haworthias, up to 20 inches. The flowers share the same white-with-brownish edging along the petals as others of the species.

Care Instructions: Water less in the summer while Star Cactus is dormant. Water more fully and regularly during the winter and spring active months, when the plant will work on offsets and leaf growth.

Watch Out For: Overwatering, not enough sun, and other typical indoor succulent challenges are important to watch for. When given adequate light and water, this plant will thrive.

Arrangement Tips: In the wild, these plants generally grow just as one rosette per plant, but, when cultivated, they will clump and fill a planter easily over time. Put a few different haworthias together for a fun "family" portrait.

HORSE'S TEETH

Haworthia truncata

HARDINESS ZONE AND TEMPERATURE RANGE
10-15; 55°F-75°F

IDEAL LIGHTING
Full sun,
partial shade

GROWING LOCATION
Indoors

MATURE SIZE
1" tall; 4"
clumping spread

PROPAGATION
Offsets, leaf;
year-round

Native to the Little Karoo region of the Western Cape of South Africa, this plant blooms between spring and summer, sending out small, long-stemmed flowers similar to its other family members. In nature, these flowers are fertilized by bees, which could explain why this plant doesn't tend to bloom much inside.

Special Features: One of the strangest-looking succulents, Horse's Teeth features rectangular leaves arranged similarly to the *Aloe plicatilis*, in two opposite rows. The plant gets its Latin name from the word *truncate*, as the grayish-green leaves look like they've been topped off, like a flattop hairdo.

Care Instructions: This plant is most active during spring and in late summer leading into the fall. Water it less during the high summer and in the winter. Its seeds are easy to germinate, and it is easy to propagate by dividing the pups. You can also propagate this plant with its leaves, but it will take months before roots emerge. Keep it dry in the meantime.

Watch Out For: Root rot and mealybugs can both be problems. Don't overwater this plant, and treat it right away if you see the fuzzy white clumps that distinguish those bugs.

Arrangement Tips: Horse's Teeth looks so interesting, it doesn't need a special pot. Perhaps terra-cotta would best highlight this unusually shaped plant. Put it in a place where you will look at it, and it may provoke philosophical thoughts.

STACKING HAWORTHIA

AKA COARCTATA

Haworthiopsis coarctata (formerly *Haworthia coarctata*)

HARDINESS ZONE AND TEMPERATURE RANGE
10-11; 50F°-90°F

IDEAL LIGHTING
Partial sun/ partial shade

GROWING LOCATION
Outdoors/indoors

MATURE SIZE
8" tall

PROPAGATION
Offsets; summer

Coarctata, native to South Africa, produces stacked, elongated leaves in rosette patterns that fit on top of one another and produce a narrow tower that looks very different from many other haworthia varietals. The leaves are green with the white tubercles that frequently define this family of plants. It has been said that Coarctata was used as a good-luck charm by warriors in the past and that it can also be used to protect you from evil spirits! I believe it.

Special Features: The small delicate flowers from the haworthia family are tubular and develop on the end of long stems that can be up to a foot long. The flowers are white and can have brown or green stripes along the petals. They arrive in late spring and can continue through the fall.

Care Instructions: Stacking Haworthia will thrive in bright indirect light. It can also take brighter sun for short periods of time but will develop reddish and purple coloring in the leaves when stressed. Water it every two weeks during the spring, summer, and fall and only once a month during the winter.

Watch Out For: Although Stacking Haworthia is able to survive in partial-sun settings, make sure it is still receiving bright light for a few hours a day at a minimum. When watering, give it a good soak; if it doesn't get enough water, it will develop a light color on its inner leaves and can eventually disintegrate.

Arrangement Tips: Stacking Haworthia's height makes it a great candidate to be planted with lower, flatter rosettes such as echeveria, graptoveria, and some sedums. It also looks great on its own in a terra-cotta pot near the window. Plant it outside with partial shade to protect from the hot afternoon sun.

RED YUCCA

Hesperaloe parviflora

HARDINESS ZONE AND TEMPERATURE RANGE
5-11: down to -20°F-45°F

IDEAL LIGHTING
Full sun

GROWING LOCATION
Outdoors

MATURE SIZE
3-5' tall: 3' wide

PROPAGATION
Offsets, root division: spring and summer

This is not actually a yucca but a member of the agave family. It has green foliage in the summer, which can turn plum-colored in the winter. The leaves have an interesting frayed, fibrous fringe along their spines. This plant is a slow grower and is respected for its incredible ability to withstand cold winters. It is found in nature from southern Texas to northern Mexico.

Special Features: Red Yucca's blooms of tubular reddish flowers crowding showy pink stalks have been known to last more than four weeks and will attract hummingbirds and bees. In warm-winter regions, these blooms can come year-round; otherwise expect them in early summer.

Care Instructions: This plant needs only moderate watering. It will want a regular drink in extreme heat or when in containers, but mostly it likes to be left alone in regions where it will get winter rain. Remove the flower stalks when the blooms have dried. It propagates best from seed.

Watch Out For: This succulent's leaves are tasty to grazing deer, so protect them when young, and enjoy the fauna when the plants are full size and out of danger.

Arrangement Tips: In desert landscapes, this is a terrific xeriscape plant. It looks great in rock gardens and grassland gardens. Plant it near boulders, and use small plants like sedums and sempervivums as companions, along with bolder plants with similarly striking flowers, like Bird of Paradise. The Red Yucca will also thrive in containers in smaller gardens, in the front of your house as a greeter, or in the back on a stone patio.

SWEETHEART HOYA
AKA VALENTINE HOYA

Hoya kerrii 'Sweetheart' or *Hoya obovata var. kerrii*

HARDINESS ZONE AND TEMPERATURE RANGE
11: 45°F–85°F

IDEAL LIGHTING
Bright light, partial shade

GROWING LOCATION
Outdoors/indoors

MATURE SIZE
Can vine up to 13'

PROPAGATION
Leaf or stem cutting: spring and summer

You may have seen this plant selling around Valentine's Day each year. Growers frequently root one bright green, fat, waxy, heart-shaped leaf in a pot—thus the sweetheart plant is born! Although we approve of a love plant, we encourage you to grow an actual plant, with its love leaves spaced out on thick, woody vines, ready to climb onto any support you provide them. The variegated varietal, *Hoya kerrii* 'Variegata', looks great, too. (All variegation is pretty much awesome.)

Special Features: Any hoya lover knows this plant is all about the flower! The star-shaped flowers come in clusters and have purple centers plastered on pearly petals. Arriving in the summer, the blooms look amazing and also have a sweet, alluring fragrance that is intoxicating.

Care Instructions: It may take a couple of years for your hoya to bloom. Don't worry, you aren't doing anything wrong. Let it get a little root-bound in its pot; that's when it will start to send out flowers. This is a semi-dormant plant in the winter, and it is more likely to flower with a little coolness and dryness during those months.

Watch Out For: Mealybugs can be a problem for a Sweetheart Hoya. Wipe them off with alcohol-soaked cotton balls, and don't forget to treat under the leaves, too.

Arrangement Tips: Kerrii loves to climb in its natural habitat. Provide your pot with a moss pole or bamboo stake and train your plant to trail upward. It will climb by itself after a short time. The sweetheart can also be a great hanging plant, with all its love leaves streaming downward.

FLORIST KALANCHOE
AKA FLAMING KATY
Kalanchoe blossfeldiana

HARDINESS ZONE AND TEMPERATURE RANGE
7-11; 40°-85°F

IDEAL LIGHTING
Partial sun to light shade

GROWING LOCATION
Indoors

MATURE SIZE
18" tall

PROPAGATION
Leaf: year-round

This Madagascar native is the most houseplant-ish member of the kalanchoe family and is an evergreen perennial. The foliage is green and bushy with waxy cup-shaped leaves that have scalloped edges.

Special Features: This plant is known for its abundance of year-long flowers, which can be red, white, orange, yellow, pink, green, lilac, or even bicolored.

Care Instructions: Once a Florist Kalanchoe's blooming period begins, it can go on for months. Multiple stems will emerge, each with 15 to 20 flowers on them. As the flowers die and dry, pinch them off. (This will frequently extend the flowering period.) Once the plant stops blooming, water a little less frequently as it tools up to begin producing flowers again.

Watch Out For: If you decide to grow blossfeldiana outdoors, bring it in during cold spells. (It does not like the cold.) Even if inside, make sure it is not getting too cold—direct sunlight will help. This is a summer dormant plant, so water less during that season. As with so many succulents, also watch for vine weevils and mealybugs.

Arrangement Tips: Because this plant is so showy, you don't have to do much to highlight it: Simply keep it in great light, water regularly, and snip the dry flowers. It will draw lots of attention wherever it lives.

LAVENDER SCALLOPS

AKA KALANCHOE STONECROP

Kalanchoe fedtschenkoi

HARDINESS ZONE AND TEMPERATURE RANGE
9–11; 25°F–85°F

IDEAL LIGHTING
Partial sun to light shade

GROWING LOCATION
Outdoors/indoors

MATURE SIZE
2' tall

PROPAGATION
Leaves, cuttings, and plantlets; year-round

Another Madagascar native, Lavender Scallops is widely enjoyed as a houseplant. Its green-blue leaves are oval with scalloped edges that turn pink or even bright red when the plant enjoys a lot of sun. The leaves have a natural variegation to them, with white undertones looking almost like a watercolor stroke streaming outward to the edge of the leaf. It is ready to reproduce at a moment's notice, rooting easily as its stems touch the soil.

Special Features: Bell-shaped pendant red-salmon flowers hang off long stems that come directly up from the leaves in spring and summer.

Care Instructions: Although Lavender Scallops loves and needs sunlight, be careful not to expose it to intense afternoon sun, as this can burn its leaves. Water less during the mostly dormant summer.

Watch Out For: Mealybugs and scale are attracted to this plant. You can treat the mealybugs with alcohol and pick the scale off the stems. If they keep coming back, you may treat the plant with one of the natural pesticides profiled in chapter 5 (page 225).

Arrangement Tips: This is a great one to plant under a tree, where it will provide color and flowers and depth to your garden, as long as it still has some sunlight. Inside, plant it in a window with blue-and-green echeveria or Zebra Plant (page 114) for contrasting patterns.

KALANCHOE 'PINK BUTTERFLIES'

Kalanchoe x houghtonii

HARDINESS ZONE AND TEMPERATURE RANGE
10–11; 30°F–85°F

IDEAL LIGHTING
Partial sun to light shade

GROWING LOCATION
Outdoors/Indoors

MATURE SIZE
3' tall

PROPAGATION
Leaf: year-round

A product of two kalanchoes that are both of the "mother of millions" variety, this Kalanchoe forms **bulbils** (see Glossary, page 237), which are little plantlets on the top edges of the leaves. The bulbils on this plant are an eye-catching bright pink and shaped like little butterflies. In most versions of this style of kalanchoe, these plantlets fall to the ground and root very quickly until you have tons of this plant—thus the name "mother of millions." However, with pink butterflies, the bulbils lack chlorophyll and cannot live on their own.

Special Features: The bright side to the bulbils not giving you new plants is that they are a vibrant, bright pink! And those pink plantlets will absolutely cover the edges of the leaves, making an extraordinary feast for your eyes.

Care Instructions: As a winter grower, Pink Butterflies likes a little more water during the fall and winter months. During the summer, you can withhold some water, as its growth slows and it cannot process it. I've heard that Pink Butterflies can produce slender pink flowers in the fall, but I have never seen any flowers on this plant.

Watch Out For: Don't overwater, and keep an eye out for mealybugs and aphids.

Arrangement Tips: Plant with other kalanchoes such as Chocolate Soldier (page 134) and Lavender Scallops (page 129) for a kalanchoe study. While their textures and colors are very different, the plants have similar needs. Plant it around agaves and other large sturdy succulents in the yard for a nice contrast.

FLOWER DUST PLANT

Kalanchoe pumila

HARDINESS ZONE AND TEMPERATURE RANGE
9-11; down to 35°F

IDEAL LIGHTING
Full sun to partial sun

GROWING LOCATION
Outdoors/indoors

MATURE SIZE
Up to 8-12" tall, but generally smaller; 2-3' spread

PROPAGATION
Stem cuttings; year-round

This is one of the smallest examples of the kalanchoe. Its silvery, purplish leaves are covered in slightly waxy white hairs, giving it a dusty look (thus its common name). It is a Madagascar native and really loves the heat, but, like so many succulents, it is also adaptable to an indoor environment.

 Special Features: Gorgeous pink-violet flowers will cover this entire plant in late winter, continuing into the spring. Roundish leaves are marginally toothed with no spines. The leaves and flowers give a great color combination.

Care Instructions: Flower Dust Plant is extremely drought-tolerant and is acceptable for xeriscaping. It is easy to propagate with leaf or stem cuttings. Cut off the dried flowers when they are done, and cut the plant back if the leaves look battered. This is a slow grower but will fill in nicely after being pruned.

Watch Out For: This plant is virtually pest-free.

Arrangement Tips: If you live in a warm climate, this is an excellent outdoor plant. It's great in beds or containers or when used to fill up any empty spaces. It's also a terrific border plant, as it will stay low and not overshadow medium-size plants, even when in full bloom. This is a fantastic indoor hanging plant, too; water it moderately and allow it to fully dry between waterings.

CHOCOLATE SOLDIER
AKA PANDA PLANT OR PUSSY EARS
Kalanchoe tomentosa

HARDINESS ZONE AND TEMPERATURE RANGE
9-12; down to 35°F

IDEAL LIGHTING
Full sun to partial sun; very hot climates might require some shade

GROWING LOCATION
Outdoors/indoors

MATURE SIZE
1-3' tall; 2-3' spread

PROPAGATION
Leaf, stem cuttings; spring

When this Madagascar native blooms, it is thought to be a sign of wealth and prosperity for the owner. It is a great outdoor landscape plant but will also live very happily indoors as long as it receives bright light.

Special Features: This succulent features little hairs on its leaves and on its blooms, giving it a voluptuous, velvety look. Its new leaves are tannish-green and edged with a reddish tint to the tips, which will turn a deep mahogany when they mature. Its flowers are bell-shaped and also fuzzy; only outdoor plants will generally bloom.

Care Instructions: Chocolate Soldier, similar to many aeoniums, loves good ventilation, so if it is inside, make sure to keep it near a window. It also likes a bit more water in the summer. Propagate it in the spring and summer by taking leaf or stem cuttings. If the leaves get dirty, use a paintbrush to gently clean them off, so as not to rub off the plant's hairs.

Watch Out For: This plant is very prone to water rot, so avoid watering the leaves if possible. It is also susceptible to rot when it is too cold, so keep it moderately warm in the wintertime. When transplanting, avoid jostling the plant's roots too much, as that may cause it to wilt right away.

Arrangement Tips: The plant's unique appearance makes it a crowd-pleaser wherever it lives. It looks terrific with almost any other succulents in a container garden. Pair it with Stonecrop Sedum (page 181) and Lavender Pebbles (page 102) for a stylized array of color.

LIVING STONES

Lithops aucampiae

HARDINESS ZONE AND TEMPERATURE RANGE
10–11, 50°F–90°F

IDEAL LIGHTING
Full sun

GROWING LOCATION
Outdoors/indoors

MATURE SIZE
2" tall

PROPAGATION
Offsets: spring, summer, and winter (not as likely in fall)

Lithops are a fascinating plant native to southern Africa. They are mimicry plants, which means they mimic the nonliving nature around them, making them look less tasty to hungry mouths. Known as living rocks, they feature two round, fleshy leaves that grow almost as one leaf, with a small space between them for a flower to push through. They come in lots of colors, and the aucampiae is a reddish-brownish color, with intricate markings on the tops of the window leaves, which are typically the only part of the plant not buried in the soil.

Special Feature: In late summer and fall, bright, yellow daisy-style flowers emerge from the space between the leaves.

Care Instructions: Stop watering Lithops almost completely during the summer, when the plant is solely focused on making a flower and can't deal with the excess water. Resume watering once the flower emerges, and continue until the flower is done and the leaves begin to dry up. Do not water again at all during the winter, as the old leaves shed like snake skin and the new leaves emerge from below.

Watch Out For: Overwatering is the main challenge with lithops. Personally, I killed about 10 of them before I understood how to keep them alive. Water twice a month at most during the watering periods. Follow this mantra: Water Lithops in spring and in fall, during summer and winter no water at all.

Arrangement Tips: Pair a Lithops only with other mimicry plants whose strange water needs are similar. Many collectors like to plant different lithops together, which looks fascinating with the different colors and psychedelic patterning on the window leaves.

LADYFINGER CACTUS

AKA GOLDEN LACE CACTUS

Mammillaria elongata

HARDINESS ZONE AND TEMPERATURE RANGE
9-11; 25°F-85°F

IDEAL LIGHTING
Full sun to bright light

GROWING LOCATION
Outdoors/indoors

MATURE SIZE
6" tall

PROPAGATION
Offsets; spring and summer

Most mammillaria are native to Mexico, like this one, which grows in the country's mountainous regions. Within the elongata varietal, there are many types and hybrids. Most feature golden radial spines that cover the long-fingered cactus (up to 6 inches per branch), giving it a lacy appearance. Ladyfinger Cactus is a clumper, like the Thimble Cactus (page 141), and it will grow along the ground and spread itself out as much as you let it.

Special Features: In the spring, bell-shaped flowers will emerge from pink buds around the top of the cactus. They may be whitish, cream colored, yellow, or pinkish, and some will have a pink stripe in the middle of the bloom. If you are lucky, they may arrive again in late summer.

Care Instructions: Like many of the North and South American natives, your elongata needs a cooling winter, with very little water. This will encourage those blooms later in the year. Even in the summer, you will probably water only twice a month, and only when the plant is dry. Make sure it has a bright, sunny spot if it lives inside; otherwise, your plant will be thinner and have less floral production.

Watch Out For: Spider mites, scale, and gnats can be a problem for this cactus. Keep an eye on your plant and pests will just be a speed bump and not a disaster.

Arrangement Tips: This can be a great hanging plant, as the offsets will grow over the sides of your planter. It is also great as a weird ground cover and looks at home in any rock and cactus garden.

THIMBLE CACTUS

AKA POWDER PUFF PINCUSHION

Mammillaria vetula subsp. *gracilis*

HARDINESS ZONE AND TEMPERATURE RANGE:
9-10; 20°F-80°F

IDEAL LIGHTING
Full sun to partial shade

GROWING LOCATION
Outdoors/indoors

MATURE SIZE
4" tall

PROPAGATION
Offsets; spring and summer

Thimble Cactus is a small clumping plant that features interlaced white radial spines covering a round green body, making it look lacy, much like the Ladyfinger Cactus (page 138). The offsets are very loosely attached, so it super simple to propagate. This Mexican native is very round in its early life, and it will grow into a more cylindrical shape over time. It is pretty easy to handle but may have one or two brownish central spines as it ages.

Special Features: There are two blooming seasons for Thimble Cactus: late winter to early spring, and late summer into fall. During these periods, creamy-white-and-yellow flowers will emerge around the top of the cactus in the crowning style that many cacti display.

Care Instructions: Outside, the Thimble Cactus can take a lot of sun and has minimal needs. Inside, provide it with some circulation. This isn't a plant that needs a lot of water. During spring and fall, water it when dry, but give it only light water in the summer; during the winter, set it in a cool spot and give it little to no water.

Watch Out For: Spider mites, scale, and gnats might be as attracted to your mammillaria as you are. Pay attention to your plants so you can hold off a widespread attack before it begins.

Arrangement Tips: This is a great houseplant cactus, as it has few needs. Provide it with a nice sunny spot and enjoy! Outside, it will make an unusual but fantastic ground cover, and it will also look great spreading in any sort of cactus or rock garden.

NOPALES

AKA NOPALITO, PRICKLY PEAR

Opuntia ficus-indica 'Burbank Spineless'

HARDINESS ZONE AND TEMPERATURE RANGE
9–11; 15°F–100°F

IDEAL LIGHTING
Full sun

GROWING LOCATION
Outdoors/indoors

MATURE SIZE
10–15' tall;
5–10' wide

PROPAGATION
Leaf, stem cuttings;
year-round

This Mexican native features oblong blue-green leaves commonly referred to as pads (actually called "thalli"). The leaves are mostly spineless and will create showy yellow-gold flowers that produce an edible fruit similar in taste to a watermelon.

Special Features: This plant is very versatile. The pads are edible raw or cooked. They can be dried to create a flour used to make cakes, squeezed to extract an anti-inflammatory gel, juiced for raw or fermented beverages, or preserved as jams and candies.

Care Instructions: An established plant needs little support. Give it some summer water in high heat (over 80°F); otherwise leave it alone. In spring, plant pads (you can even use those purchased from a grocery store) directly in the soil about a third of the way up the leaf so that your plant has time to establish before the cold months come around. It will grow in resiliency over time.

Watch Out For: This cactus is not prone to pests or disease. Make sure to remove the hairy patches of small spines called **glochids** (see Glossary, page 237) if you are harvesting the pads for consumption. You can burn them off if you are grilling; otherwise peel or scrub them with an abrasive brush under cold water.

Arrangement Tips: This is an amazing specimen plant and is great for privacy walls. It is also fire-resistant because it is so full of water. The plant is drought-tolerant and good to use for xeriscaping. Place it next to a large boulder for a dramatic effect.

BUNNY EARS CACTUS

AKA ANGEL'S WINGS, POLKA-DOT CACTUS

Opuntia microdasys

HARDINESS ZONE AND TEMPERATURE RANGE
9-11; 30°F-100°F

IDEAL LIGHTING
Full sun to light shade

GROWING LOCATION
Outdoors/indoors

MATURE SIZE
3-4' tall, slightly larger spread

PROPAGATION
Cuttings, seeds; summer

The leaves of *Opuntia microdasys* frequently come up in pairs, making the cactus look like a bunny when it is still young and sporting only a few leaves. The pretty, spineless (though very bristly) pads can grow up to 6 inches across. It's best to handle this plant with gloves and tweezers, as it will drop off the little glochids in packs in your fingers, leaving you a gift to remember it by. (Pro tip: Duct or shipping tape can help remove spines from stinging fingers.) It is native to central and northern Mexico.

Special Features: Bunny Ears Cactus makes delicate, bright yellow, bowl-shaped flowers, sometimes with a tinge of red on the margin in spring and summer. The flowers yield to reddish-purple edible fruit. In order to get them, you will need to give your plant some cool winter air in the 45°F to 55°F range.

Care Instructions: *Opuntia microdasys* will bloom in abundance if planted in the ground outside; it is less likely to bloom when grown in a pot indoors.

Watch Out For: Scale can be a problem with many opuntia. If it is potted, be careful not to overwater. Microdasys has very shallow roots and can collect its necessary water intake very easily. It should dry out between waterings and be mostly left unwatered during the winter.

Arrangement Tips: Bunny Ears is fabulous alone in a terra-cotta planter inside; it's also a great rock garden and xeriscape plant. Make sure not to plant it too close to plants that want more water.

DUNCE'S CAP

Orostachys iwarenge

HARDINESS ZONE AND TEMPERATURE RANGE
5–10; −30°F–70°F

IDEAL LIGHTING
Partial sun to light shade

GROWING LOCATION
Outdoors/indoors

MATURE SIZE
2" rosettes, will create a mat and spread

PROPAGATION
Offsets; spring

The silvery lavender coloring of this *Orostachys* is very attractive. The mother rosette throws off lots of offsets at the ends of long stems that are still attached to the mother plant. Native to mountainous regions in Japan, Mongolia, and China, this plant thrives in the warm summer and goes dormant during the freezing and snowy winter. (It is unusual for a small succulent like this to have the ability to survive a cold winter!)

Special Features: This succulent's name comes from the cone-shaped flower that grows from the center of the rosette. The flower cones can get up to 6 inches tall before they bloom in late summer with white-and-yellow flowers. Dunce Cap is monocarpic, meaning it will flower once and die. That said, there are so many offsets that this won't be disappointing.

Care Instructions: As a winter dormant plant, iwarenge survives outside by shrinking back and resprouting when the warmer spring rolls around. It does not like humidity and has a love-hate relationship with water. Its leaves will rot if they get wet while it is getting hot bright sun, so water the soil carefully. It loves some airflow during its grow seasons in spring and fall, as this helps dry the plant.

Watch Out For: Mealybugs can be a problem; give your plant regular scans. Be careful of sudden hot afternoon sun—it will burn the leaves.

Arrangement Tips: This is a fantastic ground cover, as it can survive cold winters. When many rosettes go into bloom at the same time, it looks remarkable. It is also a great hanging plant, with the offsets dangling down from the mama plant. Even alone in a window pot, it will command your attention with its unique color and style.

RUBY NECKLACE

AKA LITTLE PICKLES, STRING OF PICKLES

Othonna capensis

HARDINESS ZONE AND TEMPERATURE RANGE
9–11; 30°F–80°F

IDEAL LIGHTING
Full sun to partial sun

GROWING LOCATION
Outdoors/indoors

MATURE SIZE
4" tall with a dangle of up to 18"

PROPAGATION
Stem cuttings; year-round

Othonna capensis has long, plump bluish-green leaves on long stems that can look like little pickles, giving it one of its nicknames. It can also blush to dark red and deep purple, including the stem, in bright hot sun (hence, its other nickname). When in direct sun, the plant will be entirely purple except for its bright flowers, which give it a very striking appearance.

Special Features: Long-stemmed, plump buds open to bright yellow, daisylike flowers that can be up to 2 inches wide in the hot sun but that may not open on cloudy or foggy days. They contrast nicely with the purple foliage.

Care Instructions: This plant's gorgeous flowers will come in late spring and continue through midsummer. Removing the dead blooms will give the plant energy to continue to create new ones during the grow season. When propagating, cut a bunch of stems at one time and plant them together.

Watch Out For: Outside, a little less sun is fine, but inside, too little light can cause the plant to wither and make it susceptible to such pests as mealybugs, aphids, and spider mites.

Arrangement Tips: Outside, this can be a great ground cover, creeping along the soil. It is a great dangler and can be planted on the top of stone walls to hang downward. Inside, it is a great hanging plant for a window. It will look nice with other flowering succulents, like *Aptenia cordifolia* (page 34) with its lush, pink flowers, or any of the echeverias.

MOONSTONE

AKA SUGAR ALMOND PLANT

Pachyphytum oviferum

HARDINESS ZONE AND TEMPERATURE RANGE
10–11; 30°F–80°F

IDEAL LIGHTING
Full sun to partial sun

GROWING LOCATION
Outdoors/indoors

MATURE SIZE
4" tall with a 12" spread

PROPAGATION
Leaf; year-round

The leaves of this Mexican native are shaped like candy-coated almonds or eggs and covered in farina. They grow in pairs, facing each other, as part of loosely formed rosettes. The color of the leaves will vary greatly depending on their light and can be bluish green or grayish purple; they will even sometimes blush into the reds and yellows and oranges. While the leaves may look tasty, don't eat them; Moonstones are not toxic but still might give you a bellyache.

Special Features: Moonstone's flowers emerge at the end of their winter grow season and can be an electric red or orange. The stems can be 12 inches long and will have light green **sepals** (the leafy portion of the plant outside of the developing flowers; see Glossary, page 237) surrounding the bell-shaped blooms, which dangle down over the plant

Care Instructions: Take note—this is a winter grower with a summer dormancy period. It needs more water in the winter than many succulents. Too much summer water can lead to root rot. Give it plenty of bright morning light, but remember that hot afternoon sun can bring sunburn.

Watch Out For: Mealybugs can be an issue for Moonstone and a bummer for your farina if you have to treat it. Try not to handle those leaves if possible.

Arrangement Tips: Contrast this plant with Lavender Pebbles (page 102) and see if you can tell which is which! Alternatively, plant it with echeveria and crassula for a colorful indoor window planter. Outside, place it around large rocks and Blue Chalk Sticks (page 194) or with other pastel-colored plants.

COLUMNAR PEPEROMIA
Peperomia columella

HARDINESS ZONE AND TEMPERATURE RANGE
10–11; 50°F–80°F

IDEAL LIGHTING
Bright light to partial shade

GROWING LOCATION
Outdoors/indoors

MATURE SIZE
15" tall

PROPAGATION
Stem cutting; spring, early summer

This peperomia is named for its shape. It grows in columns, and its densely populated, horseshoe-shaped leaves fully obscure its stems. The green leaves are "windows," similar to some haworthia, which allow the sun to get to the photosynthesis cells within. The leaves become larger as they age, presenting even more space for the sun to penetrate. The stems branch regularly, making this plant sometimes look like a mound of leaves or even a wet, shaggy dog.

Special Features: Columnar Peperomia's flowers are irregular and arrive in spring, if at all. The stems are lime green and look like elongated cones or tails. Each stem is covered in tiny white or green odorless flowers.

Care Instructions: Keep your columella in bright, indirect light. Too much direct light can result in brown spots on your plant. Water moderately in the spring and summer and less during its semi-dormant winter. Mist frequently if that is part of your watering regimen.

Watch Out For: Because columella's leaves are so packed together, mealybug infestations can be difficult to remove. Try using the cotton ball alcohol method first, and if that is not working, try a watered-down neem oil spray, which the bugs hate but is organic and won't damage the plant.

Arrangement Tips: Pop this plant in a little pot with some sempervivum or low-growing sedum. Add some String of Pearls (page 61), String of Hearts (page 41), or Fishhooks Senecio (page 197) for a trailing planter. Put it in the window where you can enjoy watching the light interact with the shiny leaves.

GREEN BEAN PEPEROMIA
AKA PINCUSHION PEPEROMIA
Peperomia ferreyrae

HARDINESS ZONE AND TEMPERATURE RANGE
10-11; 50°F-75°F

IDEAL LIGHTING
Bright light to partial shade

GROWING LOCATION
Outdoors/indoors

MATURE SIZE
12" tall

PROPAGATION
Leaf cutting; year-round

Native to Peru, this delicious-looking little peperomia is coveted for its interesting foliage: Each leaf resembles a green bean (which gives it its common name). The narrow, curvy leaves appear almost folded upward and cascade down around upright stems. Where the folded leaves meet is a window, allowing the light in for photosynthesis. It is a slow grower and will probably take 10 years to reach maturity.

Special Features: The flowers on the ferreyrae are strange, somewhat resembling the columella, with long conical shapes and tiny blooms. With this plant, the stem puts out five or six of the floral cones, which can be up to 12 inches long. The tiny green-and-yellow blooms are interesting but not the main attraction of this peperomia, and many people simply clip them at the base before they even bloom.

Care Instructions: Water the ferreyrae more in the spring and summer than in the semi-dormant winter. Like columella, ferreyrae loves as much mist as you want to give it. In general, peperomia wants more water than many other succulents, but it is still in danger of root rot if it sits in wet soil for too long. It loves the sun but doesn't love too much heat, so it might be a great candidate for a north-facing window. Feel free to give it a regular pruning to maintain its bushy shape.

Watch Out For: Keep an eye on the basics: mealybugs, spider mites, and overwatering. Give this plant great airflow and regular bright light, and let it dry between waterings, and it should do great.

Arrangement Tips: Green Bean Peperomia can be a great hanging plant. It tends to be bushy and can overshadow—or even obstruct—other plants in the same pot, so consider planting it alone.

PIXIE LIME
AKA TEARDROP
Peperomia orba

HARDINESS ZONE
AND TEMPERATURE
RANGE
10–11; 50°F–85°F

IDEAL LIGHTING
Partial sun, partial
shade; won't
tolerate low light

GROWING
LOCATION
Outdoors/indoors

MATURE SIZE
3–4" tall; 3–5" wide

PROPAGATION
Leaf, stem cuttings,
root division; spring
and summer

This dwarf cultivar is native to Central and South America, where it grows under the dappled light of the rain forest canopy. There it grows epiphytically (living on other plants), with very little or no soil, on tree trunks and branches with air plants.

Special Features: This one breaks the rule: It is unusual in that it prefers higher humidity and more water than most succulent plants and, as a result, is a fantastic houseplant in most climates.

Care Instructions: The Pixie Lime wants moist soil. Water weekly, but don't leave it sitting in water in a dish. In very hot climates, mist the leaves during summer but not in winter. In warm regions, it can be grown outdoors as a ground cover in partial shade.

Watch Out For: Don't expect fast growth; this plant will stay small. It thrives tight in its little pot, so repot for fresh soil, but don't worry about planting up for growth. Though rare, it might get a virus called ring spot, which will result in distorted foliage and rings on the leaves. Destroy those plants and start again.

Arrangement Tips: Pixie Lime is nice on its own in an indoor window planter or in a hanging planter where its stems and leaves will dangle. It's also great in a wet terrarium with African violets and other high-humidity, water-loving plants.

BLUE TORCH CACTUS

AKA BLUE CANDLE CACTUS

Pilosocereus azureus 'Blue Torch' or *Pilosocereus pachycladus*

HARDINESS ZONE AND TEMPERATURE RANGE
9–11; 30°F–80°F

IDEAL LIGHTING
Full sun to partial sun

GROWING LOCATION
Outdoors/indoors

MATURE SIZE
30' tall, but not in all growing conditions

PROPAGATION
Branch cuttings, offsets; year-round

This beautiful columnar cactus comes from Brazil and is coveted for its turquoise skin, which becomes a more vibrant bright blue as it ages. As usual with succulents, the more sun exposure the plant gets, the more vibrant the color. Blue Torch also features orangish spines, which fade to a grayer tone with age and contrast nicely with the blue along the way.

Special Features: From April to July, this cactus produces big, white, funnel-shaped nocturnal flowers, which stay open for a few hours into the morning. Blue Torch can grow in hot heat, even in the summer, so don't be afraid of sunburn; make sure it gets significant indoor light as well. The more light and heat this plant gets, the bigger it will grow.

Care Instructions: Azureus is a faster grower than many cacti but will still be fine on your windowsill for many years, as it can take a while to get large and bulky. And while it can grow to 30 feet, it won't do that unless it is in the perfect growing conditions outside in Brazil. It is more likely to grow to 12 to 24 inches in a pot inside or 6 to 8 feet in most outdoor environments in the United States. It wants a bit more water than many cacti, so if it is somewhere especially hot, feel free to give it water weekly in the summer.

Watch Out For: Remove any visible mealybugs and scale. Pro tip: Wrap this plant in newspaper or brown paper when repotting or handling it at all, in addition to using gloves—its spines are no joke!

Arrangement Tips: Outside, when it gets large, a Blue Torch Cactus will eventually branch and round into a regal candelabra shape. Give it space to do its thing! Inside, put it with other cacti or give it a tall, elegant pot where it can spend its days showing off its pretty blue skin.

LOBSTER FLOWER

AKA BLUE COLEUS

Plectranthus neochilus

HARDINESS ZONE AND TEMPERATURE RANGE
9-11: down to 25-30°F

IDEAL LIGHTING
Full sun to bright shade

GROWING LOCATION
Outdoors

MATURE SIZE
1-2' tall: very wide spread

PROPAGATION
Root division, stem cuttings: spring and summer

A skunky aroma reminiscent of marijuana emanates from the neochilus, which some people will love. The grayish-green leaves are pointed, notched, and very soft. It grows faster than many succulents and will fill a planting bed in little over one season. It's native to southern Africa.

Special Features: The blooms of this plant are 3 to 6 inches tall, deep purple, and very fragrant. They might come during any of the four seasons but can be expected from spring to late fall.

Care Instructions: This is a great plant for dry locations. It doesn't need much water and will be happy receiving only winter rains. After the blooms dry, prune this plant back for appearance. This is one of the easiest succulents to propagate, so prune it regularly to maintain shape and location.

Watch Out For: This plant is not attacked by many pests; in fact, its fragrance is thought to make it repellent to deer, snails, and even snakes. The leaves will wilt when it is very thirsty, so give it a drink if you see this.

Arrangement Tips: This is a great ground cover and will look luscious when in bloom. It's lovely in hanging baskets, containers, and rock gardens. It is used for erosion control on the sides of hills because it will hold the dirt in place under its dense root system. It is a great shade plant in very hot tropical areas and a fantastic, sunny xeriscape plant in moderate temperatures with rainy winters.

ELEPHANT FOOD

AKA ELEPHANT BUSH, PORKBUSH, DWARF JADE PLANT

Portulacaria afra

HARDINESS ZONE AND TEMPERATURE RANGE
9–11: down to 25–30°F

IDEAL LIGHTING
Full sun to full shade

GROWING LOCATION
Outdoors/indoors

MATURE SIZE
8–15' tall; 4–6' spread

PROPAGATION
Leaf, stem cuttings: spring and summer

Little, roundish green leaves populate thin, brittle reddish branches on this South African native. It's not related to jade but bears a superficial resemblance, giving it the "dwarf" nickname. Tiny star-shaped pink flowers appear at the ends of the branches, only to give way to semitranslucent berries in the summer, though rarely when planted inside.

Special Features: Eaten by some humans and a lot of wildlife, this succulent's plump little leaves provide a sour tang to soups, salads, and meats. It also has strong carbon-cleaning capabilities and is known to clean the air more than other plants.

Care Instructions: This plant demands bright light and well-draining soil. Intense sun can stress the plant, turning its tips a pleasing red. But it can also cause sunburn to the leaves, so striking the right balance might be challenging.

Watch Out For: Very few pests attack this plant. Be careful not to overwater, and scan for mealybugs often.

Arrangement Tips: This plant grows naturally in rocky outcrops and sloping mountainsides, so it is a natural for rock gardens and gritty soil. In colder climates, it fills a hanging planter gloriously, with its branches spreading up and down. Because of its treelike appearance, it looks great hanging over smaller plants and fulfills the same role in open terrariums with other drought-tolerant plants.

CROWN CACTUS

Rebutia krainziana, Rebutia marsoneri 'Werderm'

HARDINESS ZONE AND TEMPERATURE RANGE
9–11; 35°F–85°F

IDEAL LIGHTING
Full sun to partial shade

GROWING LOCATION
Outdoors/indoors

MATURE SIZE
4" tall

PROPAGATION
Offsets: year-round

Argentina produces so many awesome cacti! This little clumper works as an easy houseplant as long as it gets solid sunlight and not too much water. It has round, barrel-shaped foliage and tons of little areoles, which sort of spiral into the center on the top of the plant. Clusters of small spines protrude from these areoles.

Special Features: This cactus produces early spring blooms that continue through the summer and vary from orange to red to yellow to white, with a wide array of combinations. The blooms are large and showy, especially in comparison to the relatively small plant.

Care Instructions: Let as many clusters stay with the mother plant as possible. Multiple blooms off the different foliage will look fantastic. Water weekly in the summer, bimonthly in the autumn, and only once monthly during the semi-dormant winter. Keep the cactus cool and dry during that season, as you would with other mountain-born South American natives.

Watch Out For: Scale should be removed quickly. Keep an eye out for mealybugs, too. Rebutia is mostly pest-free, but take care not to overwater it.

Arrangement Tips: Plant this alone or with other cacti in a dish. Outside, it looks great in a rock garden; it is a great xeriscape plant, like all cacti, because of its watering needs. I recommend it anywhere you have the climate for an outdoor cactus. It takes care of itself very well and gives you pretty flowers.

CYLINDRICAL SNAKE PLANT
AKA AFRICAN SPEAR, ELEPHANT'S TOOTHPICK
Sansevieria cylindrica

HARDINESS ZONE AND TEMPERATURE RANGE
9-11; 55°F-80°F

IDEAL LIGHTING
Partial sun to full sun

GROWING LOCATION
Outdoors/indoors

MATURE SIZE
12"-84" tall; spreads as much as you let it

PROPAGATION
Leaf, offsets; spring to fall

The Cylindrical Snake Plant is native to Angola, Africa. It sends out leaves from rhizomes (a type of stem that can function like a root) under the soil. The leaves are about 1 inch thick and consist of tightly banded spikes of green, with slight variegation, coming to a point at the top.

Special Features: The leaves will grow in a fan shape but are frequently sold in pots with a few propagated spears standing next to each other and even sometimes braided together. With enough light, this plant will produce a foot-long spike of aromatic white flowers edged in pink.

Care Instructions: Sansevieria is the ultimate neglect plant. Give it succulent soil and a well-draining pot and you can mostly leave it alone. Water monthly during the warm months and every other month during the winter. Keep the leaves dust-free with a moist cloth.

Watch Out For: A leaf will essentially stop growing if its point gets broken, so be careful with the tips of this plant. It may also stop growing with insufficient light, but chances are good it will still stay alive.

Arrangement Tips: This is a great container plant. Use it by itself or with Fishhooks Senecio (page 197) or another plant that will spill over the edges to provide depth to your arrangement.

SNAKE PLANT
AKA MOTHER-IN-LAW'S TONGUE
Sansevieria trifasciata

HARDINESS ZONE AND TEMPERATURE RANGE
9-11; 40°F-80°F

IDEAL LIGHTING
Partial sun
to full sun

GROWING LOCATION
Outdoors/indoors

MATURE SIZE
25-60" tall; 2" wide leaves

PROPAGATION
Leaf, offsets;
year-round

Like the cylindrical snake plant, the trifasciata is also native to Angola. The tall leaves of the Snake Plant are wide, like thick blades of swordlike grass edged in gray, silver, gold, yellow, and green.

Special Features: Give it plenty of light so that it will produce the aromatic flowers that most sansevieria are known for. It may bloom less than once in 10 years when living indoors.

Care Instructions: This incredibly easy-to-care-for plant is a favorite for offices and public buildings. Indoors, it requires a well-draining pot and will acclimate to a wide range of light, from full to very little sun. It can survive a lot of neglect, including being root-bound or water-deprived. Water every three weeks at the most during its warm growing seasons and much less during the winter. Feel free to wipe the leaves with a moist cloth to keep them free of dust.

Watch Out For: Drainage is the most important thing to keep an eye on, as this plant is prone to indoor attack by spider mites, mealybugs, and aphids. Treat accordingly.

Arrangement Tips: This plant looks fabulous in multiples in large containers. Use preserved moss like Spanish moss or sphagnum as a topdressing. Plant it outdoors in warm climates as a back border to a garden bed. Indoors, use it with other neglectable plants, like gasteria, haworthia, and cactus.

CHRISTMAS CACTUS
AKA EASTER CACTUS
Schlumbergera bridgesii

HARDINESS ZONE AND TEMPERATURE RANGE
9-11; 55°F-75°F

IDEAL LIGHTING
Bright light to partial shade

GROWING LOCATION
Outdoors/indoors

MATURE SIZE
18" tall with a 24" spread

PROPAGATION
Stem cuttings, leaf; summer, after flowers dry

Very closely related to epiphyllum plants, Christmas Cactus has leaflike growths called **cladodes** (see Glossary, page 237), which are flattened segments grown consecutively along jointed stems with notches along their edges. The long stems will eventually dangle, and flowers will bloom out of the ends of the farthest segments.

Special Features: Christmas Cactus blooms are spectacular bells, which can be magenta, yellow, red, or other colors. They first appear between November and January but can grow continuously until August.

Care Instructions: Schlumbergera needs a fair amount of darkness, especially during the period of rest between late summer and early winter. Move it to a shady place for those months. Cut back on water during this dormancy period as the plant gears up for another round of incredible flowers.

Watch Out For: Christmas Cactus doesn't like too much cold or too much water. Inside, keep it in a brightly lit spot, away from drafty windows and hot heaters. Too much water will inhibit blooms, so water moderately and make sure the pot has good drainage.

Arrangement Tips: The Christmas Cactus doesn't need anything fancy, just a nice ledge where it can hang down and delight you when in bloom or a hanging planter in a nice bright spot. If it is living outside, make sure it will be able to receive the shade it needs to resume the cycle.

BLUE ELF

x Sedeveria 'Blue Elf'

HARDINESS ZONE AND TEMPERATURE RANGE
9–11; 25°F–75°F

IDEAL LIGHTING
Full sun to partial sun

GROWING LOCATION
Outdoors/indoors

MATURE SIZE
3" tall

PROPAGATION
Leaf, stem cutting, offsets; year-round

Sedeveria is a cross between sedum and echeveria, two of the most prolific and easiest families of succulents. Blue Elf has greenish-blue leaves formed in rosettes, which closely resemble echeveria. Its leaf tips can blush from a bright pink to a deep burgundy, depending on the amount of light and water that it receives. It is easy to propagate.

Special Features: Blue Elf is known as a crowd pleaser because of the clusters of yellow five-petaled flowers that can emerge at least three to four times annually and stick around for weeks. It also grows easily removable offsets with full rosettes growing on little stems right through the leaves of the mother rosette.

Care Instructions: Caring for the Blue Elf is simple and for the most part consists of enjoying its flowers and not exposing it to frosty weather. Limit its water to help stress the plant if you want to bring out those bright colors in the leaves. Give it lots of bright light and water when the soil is dry.

Watch Out For: The usual critters, such as mealybugs and vine weevils, will attack this plant.

Arrangement Tips: This is a great option for a mixed pot with other bright colored echeveria and sedum along with a trailing plant like Donkey's Tail sedum (page 178) or String of Hearts (page 41).

CORSICAN STONECROP

AKA BLUE TEARS SEDUM, LOVE AND TANGLES

Sedum dasyphyllum 'Major'

HARDINESS ZONE AND TEMPERATURE RANGE
7-10; -10°F-80°F

IDEAL LIGHTING
Full sun

GROWING LOCATION
Outdoors/indoors

MATURE SIZE
3-5" tall; 12" spread

PROPAGATION
Stem cuttings, root division; summer

Corsican Stonecrop has miniature clusters of foliage (though bigger than the 'Minor' version) with grapelike blue-green-and-purple leaves. It will create a tight carpet as a ground cover, and the leaves will turn more purple in hot sun. Native to the Mediterranean region of Europe, it is typically found in its natural habitat growing among volcanic rocks.

Special Features: This is a fantastic cold-region ground cover. Dasyphyllum will deal with extreme temperatures in both directions. In spring and summer, this sedum will send out pink buds that will open into pretty white flowers.

Care Instructions: This sedum is very adaptable to a variety of planting locations. It can handle conditions many other plants do not like, such as very hot sun and very little water. Broken leaves will re-root where they fall, helping it spread nicely into whatever area you let it. It is super easy to propagate with divisions and also with leaves. Just replant divisions immediately, or set leaves on soil and leave them alone.

Watch Out For: Very few pests bother this plant, but like most succulents, it is susceptible to root rot.

Arrangement Tips: *Sedum dasyphyllum* is great for rock walls, in containers, between stepping-stones, and in beds around larger plants. It gives great texture and context to various-size companion plants. It is also terrific in dry terrariums with haworthia, gasteria, and cactus.

GOLDEN CARPET

Sedum kamtschaticus 'Golden Carpet' or
Phedimus kamtschaticus 'Golden Carpet'

HARDINESS ZONE AND TEMPERATURE RANGE
4-10; -30°F-75°F

IDEAL LIGHTING
Full sun to partial shade

GROWING LOCATION
Outdoors/indoors (but thrives outside)

MATURE SIZE
5" tall

PROPAGATION
Root division; year-round

This crowd-pleaser is a low-growing lime-green plant that will spread and form a thick ground cover. It is soft and pretty and soothing to the eyes. All of its parts are very small, with dainty stems and leaves and little flowers that bloom in the middle of the summer and can cover the entire plant prolifically. It's not only attractive to humans; the three *b*s—birds, bees, and butterflies—like it, too.

Special Features: Golden Carpet's flowers, which blossom for five to six weeks in the summer, are yellow and star-shaped and guaranteed to illicit "oohs" and "aahs." Even without the blooms, the plant's unique color and bushy qualities make it a great addition to your collection.

Care Instructions: This succulent wants lots of sun to get established and thrive.

Watch Out For: Don't overwater; like so many succulents, Golden Carpet requires great drainage. Inside, make sure you are giving it the most hot sun you can. Don't worry about the afternoon sun being too hot; Golden Carpet loves it.

Arrangement Tips: This is a great outdoor ground cover and can fulfil the same destiny in your indoor planter pots, so long as it is close to a bright window. It can be a good terrarium plant as long as the sun exposure is strong and you don't overwater.

DONKEY'S TAIL
AKA BURRO'S TAIL, BURRITO
Sedum morganianum

HARDINESS ZONE AND TEMPERATURE RANGE
10-11: 40°F-80°F

IDEAL LIGHTING
Full sun,
partial shade

GROWING LOCATION
Outdoors/indoors:
doesn't like extreme
heat or cold

MATURE SIZE
Trailing branches
can reach 24" long

PROPAGATION
Stem cuttings:
year-round

Donkey's Tail features overlapping, droplet-shaped, silvery light-green leaves covering long stems. This plant is native to Mexico and most likely to bloom if it's left outside.

Special Features: Flowers emerge from the very tips of the branches, opening up into fascinating star shapes of red-white-and-violet blooms. The blooms are best enjoyed if the plant is up high, as they will face downward at the end of the stem.

Care Instructions: Water Donkey's Tail moderately when the soil is dry during the active months, March to September. It is susceptible to root rot, so make sure you have great drainage and don't overwater, especially during the dormant winter months, when it needs about half the attention it gets the rest of the year. It propagates easily with stem or leaf cuttings. The leaves will live for a very long time when removed and generally will push out roots in just a few days.

Watch Out For: The leaves of this plant will pop off very easily when handled, so get it into a great place to live and then leave it alone as much as possible. Repot it rarely, and change the soil when you do. Aphids and mealybugs are the main pest concerns. Spray it down with either a low-alcohol mix (5:1 ratio of water to alcohol) or a neem oil–based mix to mitigate.

Arrangement Tips: This is a great hanging plant. Put it in a sunny spot where it won't be jostled by passersby.

COPPERTONE STONECROP

AKA GOLDEN SEDUM, SEDUM STONECROP

Sedum nussbaumerianum

HARDINESS ZONE AND TEMPERATURE RANGE
9-11: down to 30°F

IDEAL LIGHTING
Full sun to partial sun

GROWING LOCATION
Outdoors/indoors

MATURE SIZE
4-7" tall: 2-3' spread

PROPAGATION
Leaf, stem cuttings: year-round

This plant has very large leaves for a sedum: thick, pointy blades that form 2- to 3-inch-wide rosettes. This Mexican native flowers in winter through spring with mildly fragrant small white blooms.

Special Features: Coppertone has incredible color. At its dullest, it is a rusty tan with reddish pigments just below the surface. Add heat and reduce water, and the color turns vivid orange with bright red and apricot hues glowing almost translucently in the sun.

Care Instructions: Plant this in a very well-draining medium. Water moderately in the summer and much less in the winter. It can be neglected in all seasons. Coppertone tends to grow leggy in both great sun and partial sun; it can eventually be cut back and the heads replanted when they are at maximum height.

Watch Out For: You won't have to worry about many pests, but don't overwater this succulent; its color will suffer, and root rot is always a concern.

Arrangement Tips: Coppertone's bright coloring makes you want to pair it with other vibrantly colored plants like Blue Senecio (page 194), Aeonium 'Kiwi' (page 9), and Queen Victoria Agave (page 21). It's fantastic in rock gardens and containers as fill, lovely in hanging baskets by itself, and stunning against rocks and boulders of any size.

PORK AND BEANS

Sedum x rubrotinctum 'Stonecrop'

HARDINESS ZONE AND TEMPERATURE RANGE
9–11: 50°F–75°F

IDEAL LIGHTING
Full sun, partial sun

GROWING LOCATION
Outdoors/indoors

MATURE SIZE
Up to 12" high; 8–12" spread. Sends out roots along the stem and will spread out nicely as a ground cover.

PROPAGATION
Leaf, stem cuttings: year-round

Showy and colorful, Pork and Beans comes in pinks, reds, greens, and yellows. It will stress nicely; the tips can get bright in the summer and become greener in the winter. It is native to Mexico.

Special Features: This plant has pretty yellow flowers in late winter. It can withstand some colder weather but is mostly thought of as a tender plant that should avoid overwatering and extreme weather conditions.

Care Instructions: This sedum is drought-tolerant and can be mostly left alone. It should not be handled often, as the leaves will separate from the stems quite easily. Some people get a mild irritation from the sap of this plant, and it is not advised to ingest it, as it can lead to a stomachache.

Watch Out For: Pork and Beans is not known to be tasty to most pests; however, it can rot easily if it is overwatered and not allowed to dry out in between waterings. Direct sun during the winter can be detrimental to its health as well.

Arrangement Tips: This plant is great for rock gardens, and its architectural form provides height in container gardens. In outdoor gardens it will stay close to the ground around taller plants like *Graptoveria* 'Fred Ives' (page 105), agaves, and aloes. The bright, colorful leaves will contrast nicely with greener plants.

CAPE BLANCO STONECROP

Sedum spathulifolium 'Cape Blanco'

HARDINESS ZONE AND TEMPERATURE RANGE
5-9; can withstand cold down to -10°F

IDEAL LIGHTING
Full sun, partial sun

GROWING LOCATION
Outdoors/indoors

MATURE SIZE
2-6" tall; 24" spread

PROPAGATION
Stem cuttings; spring

This native of Oregon (which is grown widely along the northwestern coast) features tiny rosettes of a silvery-green color, sometimes tinged with purple. One of many sedums with the Stonecrop nickname, it is rumored to have this name because only stones need less attention and live longer.

Special Features: Cape Blanco Stonecrop will send out clusters of starry yellow flowers in the early summer. There is a hybrid version called "purpureum" that is deep purple with similar flowers and growing conditions. Some people eat it raw in salads, soups, and stir-fries. Harvest it in the morning, before it becomes more acidic. Consuming more than a handful of leaves can cause an upset stomach.

Care Instructions: When first planted, water it weekly to help roots establish. Afterward, it can be left alone with little or no irrigation. It needs great drainage to thrive.

Watch Out For: Wet areas with bad drainage will cause this plant to die back. Very few pests are known to attack it, and because it is drought- and deer-resistant, it's a desirable landscape plant.

Arrangement Tips: Plant it along rock walls, on the edges of paths, and around larger specimen plants such as agave and aeonium. Its shape and color will highlight the greens in its companion plants. It's great in dry terrariums planted with cactus and watered very infrequently.

COBWEB SEMPERVIVUM

AKA HENS AND CHICKS

Sempervivum arachnoideum

HARDINESS ZONE AND TEMPERATURE RANGE
5-8: down to -25°F

IDEAL LIGHTING
Full sun to partial shade

GROWING LOCATION
Outdoors/indoors

MATURE SIZE
2-4" tall:
8-10" spread

PROPAGATION
Offsets: year-round

Tight rosettes of green leaves covered in webbing reminiscent of a spider's web characterize this cold-hardy succulent. Frequently mistaken for an actual spiderweb, the plant's natural fiber protects it from real bugs, insulates it from the cold, and can shield it from other weather conditions, such as wind and hot sun. All sempervivums are native to the mountains of Europe.

Special Features: Like all semps, this plant features a truly spectacular bloom. The one-time-only bloom is stunning, with a thick yet soft stem extending up from the rosette and opening into an intricate array of star-shaped bright pink flowers.

Care Instructions: Keep Cobweb Sempervivum dry during the cold winter. If it is indoors, make sure it has plenty of light. Cut off and discard dead plant matter.

Watch Out For: Always prevent it from sitting in wet soil by keeping it in a well-draining pot. Provide it with some shade if it is getting a lot of hot direct sunlight. This plant is not known for pests.

Arrangement Tips: Plant it in rock gardens, directly in rock walls, along paths, in tree wells, in container gardens, in vertical gardens, and as a companion to echeveria, sedum, and other full-sun succulents.

JUNGLE SHADOWS

Sempervivum 'Jungle Shadows'

HARDINESS ZONE AND TEMPERATURE RANGE
4-10; frost tolerant to -20°F-85°F

IDEAL LIGHTING
Full sun

GROWING LOCATION
Outdoors/indoors

MATURE SIZE
6" tall

PROPAGATION
Offsets, year-round

Jungle Shadows is a cultivar introduced by Kevin Vaughn in 1969. Sempervivum—the name means "always living"—are cold-hardy plants that can live outside in some of the coldest parts of the states. Jungle Shadows is known for its reddish-purple coloring, which is blushy and rich and stays bright throughout the summer (though it can be a little greener in the hottest months).

Special Features: Sempervivum are monocarpic, meaning they flower once and then die. That said, they are so busy putting out offsets that by the time they bloom, you should have a good stash of their babies to continue your collection. The blooms are gorgeous, with spikes coming straight up through the center of the plant and opening into a cluster of pink flowers that will last for 3 to 4 weeks.

Care Instructions: Instead of trying to get your plants to bloom, enjoy them as long as you can beforehand. Jungle Shadows' foliage is pretty and will thrive with moderate sunlight and water.

Watch Out For: The pests most likely to attack your sempervivums are mealybugs and aphids. Get a nontoxic spray for the aphids and wipe away mealybugs with alcohol on a cotton ball.

Arrangement Tips: I like the combination of sempervivum and aloe and haworthia; their different colorings, textures, and shapes look great in a shared pot. A bunch of sempervivum also look fantastic outside, growing along stone walls and in cracks in the sidewalk. Take advantage of their hardiness!

HOUSELEEK

AKA HENS AND CHICKS

Sempervivum tectorum

HARDINESS ZONE AND TEMPERATURE RANGE
5-10; down to -20°F

IDEAL LIGHTING
Full sun

GROWING LOCATION
Outdoors/indoors

MATURE SIZE
4-6" tall;
6-24" spread

PROPAGATION
Offsets: spring and summer

Sempervivum is a Latin term meaning "always living." This plant earns its name by sending out tons of babies (offsets) to ensure its never-ending life. The individual rosettes will bloom spectacularly and then die (they are monocarpic). However, there will be so many rosettes that another will easily take its place. Tectorum, a common varietal of this European native, has blue-green leaves in a tight rosette with purplish-reddish highlights toward the edges.

Special Features: The one-time-only bloom is stunning, with a thick yet soft stem extending up from the rosette and opening into an intricate array of star-shaped bright pink flowers. Know that though this plant is going to die, it will leave you with a happy heart. Historically, semps were once planted on thatched roofs as a fire retardant. This is yet another reason to install a living (green) roof.

Care Instructions: Plant it in well-draining soil; water moderately. Keep it dry in winter. Remove dead flowers and rosettes.

Watch Out For: Houseleek is susceptible to crown rot but will dry some bottom leaves in an attempt to protect itself from excess moisture. It is also susceptible to endophyllum rust, an orangish fungus that will grow on the leaves of plants. Remove those leaves, and treat the plant with a fungicide, like neem oil, until all signs of the rust are gone.

Arrangement Tips: Plant it in rock gardens, directly in rock walls, along paths, in tree wells, in container gardens, in vertical gardens, and as a companion to echeveria, sedum, and other full-sun succulents.

VERTICAL LEAF SENECIO
AKA LAVENDER STEPS, LAVENDER LIPS
Senecio crassissimus

HARDINESS ZONE AND TEMPERATURE RANGE
9–11; down to 30°F

IDEAL LIGHTING
Full sun to partial sun

GROWING LOCATION
Outdoors/indoors

MATURE SIZE
24" tall; 18" wide

PROPAGATION
Stem cuttings, spring to fall

Quite different from most senecios (which are usually characterized by flexible stems and dangling foliage), crassissimus has stiff, upright purple stems with flat, glossy upturned leaves that are greenish-blue and decorated with purple edges. The leaves' interesting orientation means that when the sun is at its hottest, only a small portion of each leaf faces that heat, which protects the plant from burn and intensifies its coloring. It is native to Madagascar.

Special Features: Blossoming off a long stem, its winter flowers are bright yellow and shaped like daisies.

Care Instructions: When it reaches maximum height, which it can do in just a few seasons, it has a tendency to get floppy on top. In the spring, prune 6 to 8 inches to control it; plant the cuttings after their stems scab. Make sure this plant has excellent drainage in sandy soil, which will benefit from an annual fertilizer for nutrients.

Watch Out For: Similar to other senecios, this plant has few pests. Look out for scale and mealybugs and treat accordingly.

Arrangement Tips: The purple foliage is showy, making this a great plant in a colorful garden bed. It looks fantastic with sempervivum, aloes, sedums, and echeverias. Plant it solo in a container for an eye-catching indoor or porch plant. Since it is humidity-tolerant, it is suitable for a terrarium, but it needs to be a large one or the plant will outgrow the vessel in a year or so.

BLUE CHALK STICKS

AKA BLUE SENECIO

Senecio mandraliscae

HARDINESS ZONE AND TEMPERATURE RANGE
9-11: down to 15°F-20°F

IDEAL LIGHTING
Full sun to partial sun

GROWING LOCATION
Outdoors

MATURE SIZE
1-2' tall; 2-3' spread

PROPAGATION
Root division, leaf, stem cuttings: spring to fall

Senecio mandraliscae has silvery-blue leaves shaped like fingers curving up toward the sky. These grow from thick, ropy stems that crawl across the ground. This South African native has small white flowers that bloom in the summer.

Special Features: Blue Senecio, like many sedums and other ground cover succulents, grows tightly together, with its roots mingling to form a dense mat underneath the soil. Its bright blue leaves are coated with a dusty, chalky powder.

Care Instructions: This plant is a winter grower, like aeoniums, with dormancy during the summer. Although it is drought-tolerant, it will grow much faster with steady irrigation.

Watch Out For: Mealybugs, aphids, and spider mites like to eat this plant. Stay on it, especially during the dormant summer months. Remove dead flowers, and trim stalks regularly for appearance. Cut the entire plant way back every few years to avoid long, leggy stems.

Arrangement Tips: Blue Senecio looks great as a border plant in rock gardens and containers. The bright color complements burgundy aeoniums, orange sedums, and other bright-colored succulents. It will dangle over a container and then curve back upward, which looks especially pretty while it's flowering.

FISHHOOKS SENECIO

AKA STRING OF BANANAS, NECKLACE PLANT

Senecio radicans

HARDINESS ZONE AND TEMPERATURE RANGE
9-11; 25°F-100°F

IDEAL LIGHTING
Full sun to
light shade

GROWING LOCATION
Outdoors/indoors

MATURE SIZE
3-5" high, with
dangling stems that
can reach 4' long

PROPAGATION
Stem
cutting: summer

Native to South Africa, this plant got its name from its unusually shaped leaves, which can look like hooks or bright green bananas. They line up in single file along stems that will grow very long.

Special Features: Its tiny flowers, shaped like little puff-balls, have the unusual quality in the succulent world of having a lovely fragrance, much like cinnamon. Another senecio, String of Pearls (page 61), has a similar flower with a similar smell.

Care Instructions: Outside, it needs bright shade if it is in a hot region. Inside, it is a very easy plant to grow with plenty of bright light. Give it a lot of water during the warm months, always allowing the soil to dry between waterings. Neglect it a bit during the cooler winter. This plant is easy to propagate from stem cuttings, so whenever it needs a trim, replant the cuttings and pass along the new plants to your friends.

Watch Out For: Fishhooks doesn't get attacked by many pests, though I've seen mealybugs on it in California. Treat it accordingly.

Arrangement Tips: Fishhooks is great alone or with companions in a hanging basket. It is also a great container plant, as either a feature or one of the pack. It will act as a ground cover if you let it, crawling up the soil and rooting along the way, so it's great among rocks and pavers where you won't step on it.

PAPER SPINE CACTUS

Tephrocactus articulatus var. papyracanthus

HARDINESS ZONE AND TEMPERATURE RANGE
8-10; 15°F-95°F

IDEAL LIGHTING
Full Sun

GROWING LOCATION
Outdoors/indoors

MATURE SIZE
12" tall

PROPAGATION
Segments, offsets; year-round (segments fall off easily and are simple to root)

Native to Argentina, this *Tephrocactus* has long, soft, almost-plastic-like spines that curl a bit, like ribbons. There are also glochids around these ribbons, little hairs or spines, generally barbed, which are often found on the areoles of cacti. Don't be deceived by their harmless appearance; use gloves when handling these plants. The segments that give articulates their name are easily detached, so you will definitely have the opportunity to propagate this crowd favorite. The plant easily makes more of itself, and in its natural setting the mountainous winds regularly knock segments off the mother plant, proliferating the species.

Special Features: Paper Spine Cactus makes beautiful flowers that last just one day. These can emerge in spring, although they rarely bloom when kept indoors.

Care Instructions: This cactus can take 10 to 12 hours of direct hot sun a day, but it will also take care of itself in less sun. Water infrequently, and give it even less water if you are exposing it to less sun.

Watch Out For: Those glochids! They seem so harmless until they are spread invisibly across your hand. The plant will start to sink into itself a little when it wants water, creating horizontal ribs. (This stress is harmless to the plant and actually looks pretty cool.)

Arrangement Tips: This is another plant that looks great by itself in any planter. Pair it only with other water-averse plants. Place it in the sun for the plant's health and so you can see the light play on those weird, wide spines.

GEOMETRICUS

Tephrocactus geometricus

HARDINESS ZONE AND TEMPERATURE RANGE
9–11; 25°F–95°F

IDEAL LIGHTING
Full, hot sun

GROWING LOCATION
Outdoors/indoors

MATURE SIZE
4-5" tall

PROPAGATION
Segments or offsets; summer

Tephrocactus geometricus is a round blue-gray cactus that grows in easily separatable segments. It is native to the mountainous region of Argentina, right near the Bolivian and Chilean borders, where it receives full hot summer sun and cooler temperatures during the dry summer. It is mostly glochid-free but will occasionally have some downward-facing spines. Its shape is very eye-catching, and, as a result, your collection will receive respectful admiration. Your local nursery will likely stock this plant, but it will travel well (as most cactus do) if you order it online. Tephrocactus is closely related to opuntia.

Special Features: Geometricus makes a large, pretty whitish-pink flower in the summer that lasts only one day. It can create multiple buds per year. Luckily, the foliage is so cool-looking that the short-lived flowers won't bother you too much.

Care Instructions: Inside, you want to give Geometricus as much hot sun as possible; it is fine with afternoon heat. During the winter, make sure to withhold some water. For the blooms to come, the plant needs to be exposed to a cooler daily climate, preferably in the 40°F–50°F range. It has a thick taproot, so make sure the pot is deep enough to accommodate it.

Watch Out For: This plant can be prone to root rot. Make sure not to give it too much heat or water during the dormant winter.

Arrangement Tips: Geometricus is an "it" plant, one of those plants you see pictures of online and just have to have! Go ahead and plant it alone, then watch it create deep purple offsets. The entire plant will get darker and more colorful with extra light exposure.

NANOUK

AKA SPIDERWORT NANOUK

Tradescantia albiflora 'Nanouk'

HARDINESS ZONE AND TEMPERATURE RANGE
9-12; 55°F-75°F

IDEAL LIGHTING
Bright indirect sun to full sun

GROWING LOCATION
Outdoors/indoors

MATURE SIZE
3-6" tall, 2' dangle

PROPAGATION
Root division, leaf cuttings: spring and summer

Tradescantia is native to Central and South America, but Nanouk was actually created in the Netherlands in 2012 as a result of a (very successful!) quest to create a hardy *Tradescantia* with exquisite blooms. This gorgeous plant is a must-have if you crave color on your indoor plants. The leaves are stunningly bright and beautiful, and the flowers emerge from vibrant pink fuzzy buds! Need I say more?

Special Features: The leaves on Nanouk are magenta and green. From the top of the plant, the magenta is visible as a creamy pink that looks painted on, with long strokes alternating with green stripes and ending with a green middle and the creamy pink all around it. From underneath, the entire leaf is translucent magenta. You can see where the green stripes are, as well as light streaming through the rest of the leaf. Little yellow-and-white flowers can emerge in spring and summer, but Nanouk doesn't always bloom inside.

Care Instructions: Give it great light inside. It might sunburn if going from a shadier spot to full sun, so work that transition over a few days to acclimate it. The brightest light is necessary for bud production. Nanouk thrives in humidity, so this is another great bathroom plant. Water weekly during the summer, but make sure it is at least an inch dry before doing so. This plant grows naturally upward, so trim the tops of the stems to encourage it to branch and get bushier.

Watch Out For: Spider mites can invade if your *Tradescantia* is too dry. Trim away damaged or dying leaves to avoid welcoming them. Overwatering can be a problem; make sure your soil is dry before watering. Give the plant less water in the winter.

Arrangement Tips: You can pair this with any water-loving succulent, but it also will look great on its own in a hanging pot in the window. Add it wherever you need color in your life!

Chapter 2

SUCCULENTS AND CACTI INDOORS

Succulents love warm air and hot sun, but most of us don't have the luxury of living in that kind of climate year-round. Instead, you must adapt your care in a variety of ways to help your awesome plants survive inside. By paying close attention to their lighting source, water intake, soil composition, and air circulation, you can put your plants (and yourself as a plant parent) in the best position for success. What does success look like? For me, it means that plants are healthy and thriving and that you, as gardeners, have the knowledge and resources you need to keep them that way.

PLACING YOUR PLANTS

Succulents have evolved in extreme climates where there is a lack of regular rainfall. They've evolved to fend for themselves, and that is how we want to nurture them—re-creating these more arid native habitats and letting their natural instincts for survival flourish.

When placing new plants and planters, choose a bright, luminous spot. Plants listed as needing full sun or partial sun will want as much direct light as they can get inside. You'll want to use planters with drainage holes for your indoor succulents so that your plants don't sit in wet soil, which can bring on root rot and other problems. Our favorite families of indoor succulents are haworthia, gasteria, and aloe, all of which are partial-sun succulents with thick skin that can withstand partial shade.

If you are planting an echeveria to enjoy in your home, it should get at least four hours of constant sun. Morning sun is less hot and harsh than afternoon sun, and this will suit most of your plants.

Although they also love full sun, cacti and euphorbias will do well inside, as long as they aren't overwatered. (You can probably add 50 percent more time in between waterings for your indoor cacti than for your other indoor succulents.) Euphorbia is a plant family with many varietals that look and act similar to cacti. Their paired thorns are related to stems, while cactus spines are modified leaves. All cacti are succulents, whereas about half of the plants in the euphorbia family, like poinsettias, are not. For the purposes of this guide, when we refer to cacti, you can assume that these same directions also apply to most of your euphorbia. Make sure to identify the euphorbias in your collection and adjust your care accordingly.

Terrariums will collect and magnify heat, so place them somewhere bright but not in direct sun. The pointers in this chapter will help your plants stay happy and healthy and not get leggy or drop leaves.

CHOOSING SOIL

A funny thing about succulents is that they have a bit of a drinking problem. They don't know when enough is enough, and they can drink so much water that they form a rot under the soil that comes up into the plant. If you catch this early, you can use your propagation skills (see chapter 4) to save the plant, but the rot itself will not go away. To avoid this problem, place your succulents in a chunky, well-draining soil that doesn't hold water. Succulent soil (aka cactus soil) is widely available at nurseries and hardware stores. It is also simple to make at home by mixing potting soil with pumice or even very small pebbles. The idea is to create space in the soil for the water to run through, preventing your plant from harming itself with too much drinking.

You can add some creativity by topdressing your planting with mulch, moss, or pebbles. This will have the dual benefits of looking attractive and holding some moisture in. This won't work for plants far away from a light source (which need some sun on their soil to dry out properly), but it is a fine idea for window plantings that receive many hours of direct sun, as it can mimic the plants' natural environment.

INDOOR DESIGN BASICS

There are a lot of opportunities to be creative when planting inside. Succulents will add to the ambience of any room that has sufficient light for them to thrive. Place your container gardens in rooms that will get three to four hours of bright light, preferably from the morning sun. Consider purchasing plant lights from your local garden store or online to supplement light where it is not naturally available. This is probably the number one thing you can do to ensure that your succulents get the light they need to survive inside.

When choosing your planters, consider the basic elements of design: Color can be a fun way to connect your plants to their pots and the furniture or decor of the room. Size and scale are important so that you don't have to move something that has outgrown its location too soon. The shape of a container can be used to match plants with planters to your furniture—placing round with round or square with square creates a pleasing repetition. You should consider the texture of the plant, placing spiky plants where they can't be touched or placing fuzzy ones where they can be. And lastly, you should think about context, by which I mean you should get a feeling for your room and place plants where they can further your overall design goals. Connect your plants easily to their new habitat by matching their colors to the walls and furniture. Use a contrasting color with your planter to create a visual pop in a monochromatic room, or the opposite. Use colored tumbled glass to provide a playful topdressing in rooms with brightly colored walls.

If you want to get creative, I highly recommend experimenting with a variety of unusual containers. I've planted succulents in lunch boxes, ceramic mugs, teacups, teapots, popcorn poppers, glass pitchers, watering cans, shoes, and seashells, among other things. Find a whimsical vessel that fits your room's decor and turn it into a planter. If there is no drainage, and it doesn't make sense to drill or cut holes in it, use some drainage rock and **horticultural charcoal** (see Glossary, page 237) to separate the plants from the water. You can also put decorative elements in the containers with your plants. Arrange chunks of colored glass, metal figures, or favorite shells on top of the soil as companions to your plants. Just remember, your plants are alive, so consider their growth potential when placing them.

POTTING AND REPOTTING

Changing the container for your plant is a part of plant parenthood. You may have a new plant in a plastic pot or a well-loved one that has outgrown its planter, or maybe you have a bug infestation that requires completely new soil. Not only is this sometimes necessary, it is also rewarding. When choosing your planter, weigh a few factors:

▶ Make sure the pot you pick has a drainage hole and a dish for underneath the plant so that water doesn't leak all over your table or floor.

▶ Choose a container whose color, shape, and design will complement the plant it will hold.

▶ Succulents like to grow to the size of their planter, so pick something that reflects your desired size for the plant.

Now that you are ready to pot, follow these steps:

1. Gather your materials somewhere easy to clean—a back deck or kitchen counter will do—or cover a table with some paper or an old tablecloth.

2. Give your new pot a good wipe to make sure it is fresh and ready.

3. Cover the bottom with drainage rock, and if you have it, add a few teaspoons of horticultural charcoal, a great maintenance tool for any succulent planting. Add a few inches of succulent soil to the bottom of your planter.

4. Now move your attention to the current planter. If you have any top-dressing, carefully shift that off into a separate bowl or dish.

5. Use a flat trowel, or even a butter knife, to go around the edge of the planter to loosen the plant. Tip the pot at a slight angle and, holding the base of the plant, slide it out of the planter. It is possible the entire plant and full root ball will come up. If that is the case, slide it right over into the new vessel. If not, add more soil to the new planter so that your plant will sit at the right height in its new home.

6. At this point, check to see if you put enough soil, or too much, down at the bottom of your new planter. If it's too much, lift the plant and remove some soil so that it sits in the planter a little below the rim. If there isn't enough, add more soil below the plant and around the sides to bring the plant up to the right height. Press down with your fingers until the soil is compacted and completely filled in. Now your plant is ready for new growth and expansion.

Note: If you are working with a cactus, don't just grab it with your hands; most cacti will leave you with a painful memento. Use leather garden gloves if you have them, or cut up a paper bag and wrap it around the cactus before you gently lift it.

WATERING AND FERTILIZING

All living things need water, and succulents are no different. But we must keep in mind their propensity to drink too much and give them only what they need. For the most part, the smallest plants need to be watered every 7 to 10 days, decreasing the frequency as they get larger. Even more importantly, they want to be dry before you water again. Touch the soil: Is it moist at all? Leave it alone. Is it dry at least 2 inches down? Time to water.

When your succulent is thirsty, you will see its leaves start to pucker, like fingers and toes after a bath. Unfortunately, the main sign of overwatering is rot, and often when you first notice, it is too late. With both over- and underwatering, you may see yellowed leaves. (This can also mean that your plant has used all the nutrients in its soil and needs to be repotted.) Get on a regular watering schedule that follows the seasons, and stick to it. In general, water every two weeks in the spring and summer, but only when the soil is dry. But make sure this aligns with your plant's grow season.

During the winter months, drop down to every three to four weeks. When watering a plant with a dish below it, make sure you empty the dish after it drains.

You can also use fertilizer to keep the soil fresh and the plant happy. We generally recommend fertilizing twice a year: during early spring to encourage those flowers, and during fall in anticipation of the harsh winter. I like to use an organic liquid fertilizer that is high in calcium, which succulents love. Be sure to follow the manufacturer's instructions carefully. Too much fuel is not good for plants, so just give them what the maker suggests.

MAINTAINING YOUR PLANTS

Whether through a regular watering schedule, sun nourishment, fertilization, or just a little trim every now and then, we must care for the living things around us lest they become fallow. Succulents will drop leaves for a variety of reasons. Once you see a leaf drying up, it is fine to pinch it off with your fingers or snip it with sharp scissors. If your plant is getting huge, you might decide to repot it, propagate it, or just manicure it. When I am having a problem with my plants, I frequently move them around my house to find the right spot for them. Maybe they are getting a little too much sun, or not enough.

If you notice a soft, wet spot on the stem of your plant, this is a sign of rot and you must deal with it quickly. Cut the plant about a half inch above the wet spot. The wet spot and the rest of the plant below it, including the soil, can be removed from the pot and discarded. Follow the propagation instructions in chapter 4 to root and regrow your plant from the cutting you have taken.

Chapter 3

SUCCULENTS AND CACTI OUTDOORS

In this age of climate change, outdoor succulent gardens can provide you with so much beauty while also offering easy maintenance—without requiring a lot of irrigation. Many of these drought-tolerant plants will need nothing more than some minor weeding and trimming but will provide you with offsets, gorgeous flowers, and the companionship of hardy flora. There are lots of succulent plants that will thrive outside, and with access to more sunlight, they will "stress" into deeper and richer colors. If you have the space, time, and energy (and the right climate), you can have a stunning succulent garden that will be the envy of your neighbors.

PLACING YOUR PLANTS

As you take a look at your yard and ask yourself where your plants should go, there are a number of considerations to keep in mind:

▶ Where does the sun cross the yard? Make sure to locate the direct sun, partial sun, and shade areas for your planting plan.

▶ Are there already planting beds established in the yard? If so, make sure to augment the soil for succulents if necessary. You can augment with pumice if the soil is dense but not rocky. Succulents want water, but they also want it to drain away after they get a good drink. I mix two parts potting soil to one part pumice for my succulent soil blend.

▶ Where can a plant be placed to grow large over time and not be in the way? This is where to plant agaves, large aloes, cacti, and euphorbia.

▶ What are your plans for long-term growth? Leave room for that expansion around your plants.

▶ How hot and cold will it get year-round in your yard? Make sure to use plants as cold hardy as necessary for your zone, and also choose ones that can take as much sun and heat as they might get in that location.

Since succulents are sun-worshipping plants, light is a crucial consideration.

Remember, all "full-sun" areas are not created equal. Full sun in a place where the temperature can reach 95°F will be quite different from full sun where it never surpasses 75°F. Take this into consideration to avoid sunburned leaves when placing echeveria, graptoveria, aeonium, and other "moderate" full-sun plants. (These like direct sunlight but not when the heat is extreme—say, 90°F or above.) Look at the plant profile to see if your flora likes a little shade, too.

CHOOSING SOIL

Succulents require excellent drainage to survive. They don't like soil that will hold water; instead, they want the water to come through, allowing their roots to drink what is necessary and then move on. To test your soil for drainage, dig a hole 1 foot deep and 1 foot wide and fill it with water. If the water doesn't drain within 30 to 45 minutes, you will need to augment the soil. Succulents don't want to be coddled, so even if you have a well-nurtured planting bed in place, you still may need to add succulent soil, or even just pumice, vermiculite, or sand, to what you already have. Certain challenging soils like clay may require a deeper hole to be filled with a couple inches of pumice below your plants. Rough, rocky soil should be fine.

Topdressing is a good way to create eye-catching succulent displays. Mulch can be very helpful by providing a neat, organized look; it also supports plants in very hot locations by preventing water evaporation and eventually breaking down to augment the soil with nutrients. Use large rocks and boulders as a topdressing to hide rocky, clunky soil and to provide structure and scale to contrast with and accent your plants. Smaller pebbles will complement more colorful succulents as they rise like a tableau from the garden floor. Try using different-colored pebbles in different locations for a stylized look.

OUTDOOR DESIGN BASICS

When planning your outdoor garden, decide how much space you will allot to your plants. Seating areas can help delineate or punctuate your garden into zones. It might be nice to have one spot where a group of people can sit and a smaller spot for peaceful meditation. Make sure these areas have the best views of your garden and the world beyond. Incorporate the colors and shapes of the plants, furniture, walls, and fences that are there into your design. Let some of your plant and/or planter decisions be guided by these shapes: Use square planters where lines are sharp; choose round plants and planters where you have soft curves and oval patterns.

Scale is important, so select plants that will still be appropriate for the space once they've reached their maximum size. Don't add plants that will get very large to a small space, unless they are the focal point with a few smaller plants around them. Landscaping lights can really make your garden pop. Add them judiciously; with evening light, less is more. Set them on a timer so that they will come on and off independently.

Use rocks, water features, sculptures, and hills to create spaces within your larger space. Plant in patches around a central path through the garden, using larger, bushy succulents like aloe, kalanchoe, and aeonium to make borders around patios or along fences. Adding stone, wood, and metal elements to your design will add dimension and round out your space. For example, you can topdress your planting area with stones of different sizes and shapes to make a basic rock garden. Add a fountain or pond to promote tranquility. Plant sedum ground covers along paths and between stepping-stones. Consider a vertical garden if your space is full and you still want some succulents outside.

PLANTING

Now that you're ready to create a succulent garden, gather your materials. You'll need:

▶ A good shovel

▶ A trowel

▶ Gardening gloves

▶ Some buckets to house the soil you dig out

▶ Compost bags for any other detritus

▶ Gardening scissors for manicuring

- ▶ Your new plants

- ▶ Mulch or other topdressing

- ▶ Optional: a larger rock or two to create ambience around your plants

- ▶ Other optional materials: a water bottle, good music or a podcast to listen to, and, hopefully, a friend to share the work

Before you begin, have a good design prepared, along with an implementation plan. Know where each element will go, based on the considerations we discussed earlier in the chapter, such as where the sun shines and which plants will get large and which will stay small. Set the plants down in their spots, and view the layout from different perspectives to see how it looks. Be flexible; sometimes a plan needs to be adjusted for design or to accommodate surprising changes to plants' structure or size. Start planting toward the back of your bed and work your way forward. Enjoy the process; you are designing an area of beauty to appreciate for years to come.

When planting individual succulents, dig a hole a little bigger than the plastic planter your plant is in. Plan on sprinkling some succulent soil or pumice into the hole before you put your plant in. Remove the plant from its pot, and pull and tug a little at the roots to disrupt them a bit, which will encourage new growth once it's planted. If it is a large plant, use your scissors on both sides of the root ball and make several cuts into the roots on the

outer edge. Set your plant in the hole and fill it with succulent soil. If compatible, use some of the soil you dug out. Pat it down firmly, then repeat the process until all your plants are settled.

WATERING AND FERTILIZING

When you initially plant your succulents, don't water them for the first week, then give them a good soak. Regular watering may be less crucial later, depending on where you live and how much rain you get. If you live in a moderate climate with a mild but active rainy season, it may not be necessary at all. If you live in a very hot, dry climate, water your plants about twice a month during the spring and summer, and monthly during the winter. Most succulents will be fine if watered with a hose on a shower setting. Spend 5 to 10 seconds watering the soil around them. Because they are fragile, your littlest plants will prefer either in-ground irrigation or a gentler hose setting. In general, water in the early morning or in the late afternoon, before or after the hottest times of the day. Watering during the heat will waste water, as some will evaporate before the plants even have a chance to drink it.

Many succulents don't require any fertilization. If you want to fertilize in a moderate climate, the two seasons I recommend doing so are in the fall, to help fortify the plants for the winter, and in early spring, to incentivize those gorgeous succulent flowers we are always waiting for.

In hotter climates, it is more important to fortify the plants. If you want to use a chemical fertilizer, find something organic, with a ratio of 5:5:5 or less. This refers to the percentages of nitrogen, phosphorus, and potassium in the mix. You can also use a standard seaweed fish emulsion fertilizer, which has all the nutrients succulents need. (I frequently use half the amount of fertilizer that is suggested.) Plants like food but they don't want to be overfed, and too much fertilizer can sometimes be the source of browning leaves. Once or twice a month during their growing cycle, usually spring and summer, should be enough. Don't feed them when they are dormant; they can't digest while they are hibernating.

MAINTAINING YOUR PLANTS

When thinking about the maintenance of your plants, decide if you prefer a natural "wild" look or a more manicured one. If you like your nature natural, maintenance will involve watching for bugs and weeds and trimming dead leaves and flowers. If you want your garden to be very organized, you will be trimming and pruning as well.

Some succulents, such as Blue Senecio (page 194), have a defined growing season, and those plants will want to be cut back each winter to promote fresh, healthy growth. When your succulents bloom, you will have to trim the dead flower spikes after they have dried. Pull weeds that come up around your plants, taking care to get the roots if you can so they won't come up again. Mulch will help keep weeds away over time. Watch for infestations and fungal infections, and treat them accordingly. Succulents are relatively pest-free, so those problems will be the exceptions, not the rules.

Once your plants are established, you will get lots of new growth, which you can enjoy as is. You can also choose to propagate those plants; soon you'll have many more plants to put around your yard, plant in containers, or give as gifts to friends and family. Most offsets are easily removable from the mother plant and will readily take root in a separate container. See chapter 4 for more information about propagation.

Best Succulents and Cacti for Colder Climates

Most succulents and cacti prefer USDA zones 9-11, where there is enough warmth and sun and not too much rain. Most of the plants listed here have originated in mountain climates around the world, where they have warm weather during the spring and summer, and dry, cold weather during the fall and winter, when they go into a dormant or semi-dormant state. Some of these may appear to die back completely in the snow but will bounce back in the spring. For those of you living in zones 5-8, here are some great cold- and wet-tolerant succulents:

Parry's Agave	*Agave parryi*	*page 18*
Queen Victoria Agave	*Agave victoriae-reginae*	*page 21*
Silver Dollar Jade	*Crassula arborescens*	*page 49*
Hardy Ice Plant	*Delosperma cooperi*	*page 62*
Red Yucca	*Hesperaloe parviflora*	*page 122*
Nopales	*Opuntia ficus-indica 'Burbank Spineless'*	*page 142*
Dunce's Cap Succulent	*Orostachys iwarenge*	*page 146*
Corsican Stonecrop	*Sedum dasyphyllum 'Major'*	*page 174*
Pork and Beans	*Sedum x rubrotinctum 'Stonecrop'*	*page 182*
Cape Blanco Stonecrop	*Sedum spathulifolium 'Cape Blanco'*	*page 185*
Cobweb Sempervivum	*Sempervivum arachnoideum*	*page 186*
Houseleek	*Sempervivum tectorum*	*page 190*

Cobweb Sempervivum *Sempervivum arachnoideum*

Chapter 4

PROPAGATION

Anyone obsessed with succulents will agree that propagation is where fascination becomes enchantment. The fact that you can create so many plants from just one plant is beyond rewarding—it is shrewd and clever as well. A succulent's strong will to live and accommodating nature is never as apparent as when you propagate it. By mastering just a few of the techniques outlined here, you can grow your collections almost infinitely. Whether you are working with cuttings, leaves, division, offsets, or seeds, propagating your succulents will let you easily turn one plant into more simply by adding a little time, sun, and water.

CUTTINGS

Many varieties of succulents can be propagated by snipping a little piece off the mother plant where there are new stems and growths. The piece you have removed is called a "cutting" or "stem cutting." This is the quickest and most immediately gratifying way to multiply your plants.

Since succulents have difficulty monitoring their water intake, we let our new cuttings dry on a tray with bright light for at least a week. During this time, they will scab over where they were cut and possibly even start to send out little roots. The scab will prevent the plant from taking in too much water when planted, and the roots will reach out for nutrients when the plant is situated in the soil.

When ready, you can place the cuttings in a planter with fresh succulent soil or directly in the ground outside. Don't water for the first two weeks; this will encourage the growth of roots to help your cutting establish itself in the soil. Afterward, regular waterings will encourage the plant to grow and thrive.

Cuttings are especially great for constructing certain types of vertical gardens planted in moss. Aeoniums, kalanchoes, crassulas, senecios, and some other succulents that grow offshoots are perfect candidates for this type of simple propagation.

LEAVES

Leaf propagation is succulent magic! Many varietals, such as echeveria, graptoveria, and graptopetalum, will reproduce entirely from just one leaf. Succulents are the ultimate "will-to-live" plants; they don't want to die, and they will prove that to you by reproducing leaf by leaf.

Separate a leaf from the mother plant as cleanly as possible (they will usually just pop off in your fingers). Lay the leaf on a tray in a dry, bright environment. After a few days, you may see the first little hairy red roots sprouting from the leaf. This is an indication that your leaf is expressing its strong will to live.

After you get some roots, place the leaf on a bed of soil in a planter or on a tray, curved-side down and in a dry environment, and mist it with water every week. If your leaves are outside, make sure they are protected from the rain and not in direct sun.

Soon a miniature rosette will sprout from the base of the leaf. Now you can water it every two weeks, with just enough water to moisten the soil. Succulents prefer a little neglect over too much nurturing.

Wait until a rosette is at least 1 inch wide before repotting. For most succulents, this will take four to eight months. Plant it with succulent soil in a pot with a drainage hole.

DIVISION

Many succulent plants multiply by sending out roots along the underside of their stems that connect with the soil and allow the plant to spread out along the ground. Sedums (succulent ground covers), senecios (generally known for their gorgeous dangling tendrils), and crassula all exhibit this type of growth. These plants can grow in bushy, low clumps and are easy to separate into many plants.

First, take the plant out of its planter. Holding the plant in your hands, with your thumbs closest to you, gently use your fingers to open the plant outward, separating it first into two parts and then into as many parts as you'd like. The plants will end up in small clumps with shallow, feathery roots slipping down into the soil.

Each of these clumps can be replanted, either separately in new pots or together in a centerpiece to highlight a larger plant. I find this to be especially fun when creating terrariums: Separate a sedum into three or four clumps and then plant them around cactus and haworthia for an elegant and manicured look.

OFFSETS

Have you heard the term *hens and chicks*? It is used to describe certain types of succulent plants, generally in the echeveria and sempervivum families, that reproduce with offsets surrounding a main plant. The "hen" is the mother plant, and the "chicks" are its little offsets, sprouting up around Mom, connected with little stems much like umbilical cords. Aloes, haworthias, agaves, and gasterias also reproduce in this way, sending chicks (also known as pups or offsets) out into the world.

Interestingly, many of these plants will not reproduce using leaf- or stem-cutting methods. However, the offsets are quite easily separated from the main plant and just need a little water and sun to grow into mature plants of their own. Repot if you wish once they are 1 to 2 inches tall. If only human children were this easy!

SEEDS

If you have seeds, either from a package or from flowers that you have dried, you have the opportunity to produce many plants at once, although this is a more challenging way to propagate succulents.

Succulent seeds need soil and lots of light to germinate. They tend to be very small, so it can be easy to lose track of them when you are planting. For the best results, follow these basic steps:

Get a seed tray (sold at garden stores), or use an empty egg carton. Fill it with a nice blend of succulent soil, heavy on the pumice, to about ½ inch below the top of each opening. With clean, dry hands, place your seeds right on top of the soil. Don't worry about digging them in. Cover your seed tray with the lid; if you are using an egg carton, cover it with some plastic wrap.

One concern with this method is losing the tiny seeds before they sprout. I find this to be a challenge when watering, because they can swim away with the runoff, so I like to place the tray in another larger tray filled with water and let the soil absorb the water from below.

Keep the soil moist as the seeds grow and develop, and make sure they have either bright indirect sun or grow lights at least 12 hours a day. Most succulent seeds will start to germinate within three weeks (though some can take much longer). Soon they will start to grow little stems and leaves. Once you can see their leaves start to plump, let the soil dry between waterings.

Pot the plants up individually, or in groups of three, in fresh, well-draining succulent soil when they are 2 to 4 inches tall, or when their rosettes have developed to around that same size. Cacti can be potted when they are smaller.

This process is slow and can be relatively challenging (especially compared to the many other ways of multiplying your plants), but if you get good at germinating succulent seeds, you can easily have a ton of succulents for just a little money spent.

Chapter 5

TROUBLESHOOTING COMMON PROBLEMS

Your job as a plant parent is to take good care of your plants. There are a lot of problems that can occur, and most of them are easy to deal with. In this chapter, I lay out the most common issues you may encounter and arm you with the knowledge to identify those problems and correct them.

The three main factors that encourage healthy plants are water, light, and airflow. The plant profiles in chapter 1 highlight when one of these factors may be more important for a specific plant. Otherwise, remember: Succulents are sun worshippers that need water only when they are dry and like a moderate airflow to keep from getting damp and humid. If any of these things is off, it can open the door to pests and disease. Make sure your succulents are in the right environment to thrive.

USING INSECTICIDES

Some plant problems may require you to use a pesticide of some form. When this is necessary, I recommend using an organic and nontoxic formula as often as possible. We have only one planet, and it is up to us to protect it from harmful chemicals. Here are short descriptions of several natural pesticides that we regularly use in the shop:

Insecticidal Soap: These soaps are generally appropriate for organic gardening and designed to kill scale, aphids, white flies, grasshoppers, earwigs, spider mites, thrips, and other common pests. Because insecticidal soap is also a fungicide, you can also use it to contain powdery mildew. Spray it on your plants weekly or biweekly while you are dealing with an outbreak, and it eliminates pests on impact. My favorite insecticidal soap, made by Bonide, is safe enough to use on edible plants, even on the day you are harvesting.

Neem Oil: Extracted from the seeds of the neem tree, this oil has been used medicinally by humans for more than 4,000 years. It is a natural pesticide and helps deal with caterpillars, mealybugs, scale, spider mites, aphids, and beetles. It is especially effective against the baby and larval stages of these pests. It is sold diluted, as a spray, or by itself as a stinky oil that you can easily mix with water and a little bit of dish soap (which serves as an emulsifier) to make a pest-repellent spray of your own.

Rubbing Alcohol: Isopropyl alcohol is a great resource in your battle with succulent pests. It kills most on impact, and it leaves no real lasting effect on your succulents. After you've controlled the outbreak, you may need to spray the entire plant with water to clean off the residue left behind by the rubbing alcohol. You can use the alcohol as a spray or wet cotton balls with it and rub the pests off your plant's leaves and stems. Either way, you should dilute it halfway with water before application. If spraying, make sure to spray the whole plant, and maybe any plants in the surrounding area. Spray the soil, too, to get any eggs that have been left behind.

COMMON PROBLEMS AND THEIR SOLUTIONS

While almost every issue is resolvable, keep in mind this one caveat that all plant lovers need to remember from time to time: Plants are replaceable, and sometimes you need to recognize when keeping them alive is more trouble than it is worth. There are moments when you just have to nod your head and tell yourself you did the best you could. There is no shame in that. That being said, let's arm you with the skills needed to take care of your plants.

PLANT IS GETTING LEGGY

Likely cause: The plant is positioned too far away from the light source
Solution: Reposition the plant in stronger light as soon as possible

The technical term for this problem is *etiolation*, which refers to uncontrolled growth and chlorosis, a yellowing of the foliage. Succulents that require a lot of sun will seek it out if they are not receiving enough. You see this especially with indoor succulents, such as echeveria, graptoveria, crassula, cotyledon, haworthia, and other rosette-based plants. These plants will literally stretch their stems and leaves toward the sun, bending or lengthening the plant in the direction of the light.

If your plant has already grown out of its normal shape, repositioning it will not change the new shape of the plant, but you have a few options: First, you can top the plant and propagate the rosette. That will solve the shape problem and, if all goes well, continue the growth of your plant. Second, you can enjoy the strange new shape. There is no rule as to what your plant must look like. Avoid comparisons to collections you see elsewhere; if you are enjoying your plant, give yourself permission to do just that.

PLANT IS DRYING AND SHRIVELING

Likely cause: Too much light, or a seasonal dormancy
Solution: Move your plant farther from its light source

If your plant is getting too much light, it might react by shrinking back. *Dormancy* is when a plant is reserving its

energy and no longer growing. During those periods, most succulents need much less water and even cooler temperatures. They also will sometimes appear to dry up and shrink.

If you move your plant farther away from the light source, it might bounce back quickly. Don't move it into a dark spot; every succulent needs a certain amount of daily sun, and it will definitely not survive without it, even in dormancy. If your plant is simply dormant, it is nothing to be alarmed about. Stay calm and begin watering it again in its next growing season and watch it reanimate.

DRYING QUICKLY AFTER WATERING

Likely cause: Needs to be repotted
Solution: Get a larger pot and transplant

Plants are nourished by the nutrients in their soil. Over time, succulents can become rootbound and essentially finish the nutrients in the dirt. At that point, a larger pot and fresh soil are needed so that the plant has nutrients and room to grow. Remove your plant from the pot, and discard the old soil. You can even brush away any soil attached to the roots of the plant. Fill a pot that is a few inches larger than the last one with succulent soil and gently situate the plant and its roots into the new soil. Wait a week to water as the roots explore their new environment and reactivate.

THE LEAVES AND STEMS ARE DROOPING AND SAGGING

Likely cause: Overwatering, or just getting long enough to dangle
Solution: Cut back on watering for a week or replant in a hanging pot

Sometimes when you overwater, the plant starts to sag under the weight of the water. This may also be accompanied by dropping lower leaves. Pull back on your watering and see if the plant stands straight again. If it is still drooping, make sure it is getting enough sunlight.

Some succulents are danglers and need to get a certain size to start hanging down. If this is one of those (check the plant profiles in chapter 1 to find out!), there is no problem with your plant; just get ready to transplant it into a hanging planter and enjoy its new shape.

BROWN, GREEN, OR BEIGE BUMPS ON STEMS, OFTEN ACCOMPANIED BY A STICKY NECTAR

Likely cause: Scale
Solution: Treat with isopropyl alcohol, scrape off the scales, and apply pesticide

The term *scale* refers to around 8,000 species. Even mealybugs are a type of scale. Here we are talking about the soft-bodied or armored scale that are most commonly found on your succulent plants. The males can generally move around during their two to three days of life, but the females will press their heads into a stem or the underside of a leaf and remain there, feeding on the sap of the plant. Plants infected with scale will secrete a sticky substance, called honeydew, which resembles tree sap and causes other problems such as sooty mold (a black fungus that will form on the honeydew).

Your plant may start to look weakened and drop yellowed leaves when it is being attacked by scale. It will also eventually die if you don't treat it, and the surrounding plants are also in danger if the affected plant isn't isolated. Spray the plant down with isopropyl alcohol, then scrape off the scales gently with your thumb. Use a pesticide such as neem oil to keep them from coming back. Always remember to check the surrounding plants.

WHITE CLUMPS ON OR NEAR THE BASE OF THE LEAVES

Likely cause: Mealybugs
Solution: Remove with rubbing alcohol or pesticide

Mealybugs, a form of scale, look like a little powdery clump on the stems and leaves of plants. Like the other scale pests, they suck the juice from your plant, diminishing its strength and sometimes killing it. Use cotton swabs and either rubbing alcohol or a neem oil spray to clean them off. Treat the entire plant to protect against some mealybugs you don't see, including their larvae, and to prevent them from finding a safer place to live on your plant. Many pests will lay their eggs in the soil, so with large infestations, always repot with fresh soil during the treatment.

WHITE POWDER FORMING ON THE LEAVES

Likely cause: Powdery mildew
Solution: Treat with insecticidal soap and increase airflow to limit humidity

This is a fungal infection. It generally occurs in warm and damp environments, much like root rot (which is much more fatal). Powdery mildew can be treated with an insecticidal soap. You can also start watering early in the day to prevent a wet evening environment. Create more airflow around your plants, with a small fan, to disperse humidity. Note: You should isolate or destroy a plant that has a large outbreak. You don't want it to spread.

HOLES IN LEAVES

Likely cause: Snails or slugs
Solution: Find and remove the pests, possibly add copper tape

These common garden pests are large enough to spot easily, and you can simply pull them off and move them. They will probably be on the underside of a leaf. If they keep coming back, wrap the planter with copper slug tape (available at most garden stores). The pests won't cross the copper and won't be able to get to the leaves they want to eat.

WET SPOTS ON THE STEMS

Likely cause: Root rot from overwatering
Solution: Cut back on watering completely until you determine if the plant is salvageable

This is probably the number one problem for new succulent collectors. It is also totally normal, because most plants want to be watered more than succulents, and part of our loving nature is to nurture things. With plants, that can mean a little water every time we stop to admire a green friend. Even with non-succulent plants, that approach is not healthy. If you are unsure when to water, make a schedule, using a calendar or your smart phone, that will remind you when your plant is ready for more. No plant, or any living thing, wants food randomly and without order.

With succulents, it's better to underwater than overwater. Underwatering may result in a weakening of the plant, but that is generally reversable. Overwatering creates root rot, which is a fungal infection that attacks the roots. This infection starts underground and works its way up through the stems of the plant. Wherever you see it, that part of the plant is not recoverable. Take cuttings from the plant above the mushiness and propagate those pieces. Throw away the infected plant, including the soil. Keep in mind, most succulent plants want water only after they have dried completely or at least a couple inches down into the soil. Most succulent plants, in solid proper light, will be dry a couple weeks after each watering. (Adjust this schedule for dormant seasons.)

COLORFUL LEAVES TURNING GREEN

Likely cause: Not enough sun, too much attention (meaning too much water, nutrient-rich soil, and/or fertilizer)
Solution: Give the plant less attention to bring back those pretty colors

A lot of the prettier, more colorful succulents need a ton of sun to keep those colors vibrant. Outside, it's a little easier to get that exposure. Inside, it can be challenging. If the plant is healthy, this may not be a problem. Fading back to green may not be desirable, but it is hardly reason to give up on your plant. Put your plant in a brighter spot if you want more color, or leave it where it is and enjoy the darker-green coloring.

THE LEAVES ARE CURLING OR MISSHAPEN AND ARE YELLOWING AND STICKY

Likely cause: Aphids
Solution: Treat with insecticidal soap or neem oil and repot

The nice thing about aphids is that they are pretty easily identified. They look almost like very tiny grasshoppers, and they like to hide along stems, under leaves, and in the curled-up spots on leaves. You can take a photo and zoom in to confirm. Like many other pest insects, they like to eat your plant, which weakens it and can also kill it. Treat them with insecticidal soap or neem oil, and if it is a big infestation, definitely repot the plant because their eggs are probably in the soil. If they are all over the plant, discard it and make sure the plants near it are not infested as well.

SPIDERWEBS AND DUSTY LEAVES

Likely cause: Spider mites
Solution: Treat with insecticidal soap and clean off the webs

Spider mites thrive in very dry situations. You may see them where your plant has drying bottom leaves or anywhere on the plant during a dry dormancy period. They can be controlled with natural predators, such as ladybugs. They should be controlled as soon as you notice them, before they make the jump to all your other plants. They attack in the same way as many of the pests, by sucking the juice from inside the plant. Use insecticidal soap and clean off the webs with rubbing alcohol and cotton balls. Pay close attention to any plants that show these symptoms, and treat them weekly or biweekly. If you are unlucky and your aloe plants are attacked by spider mites, you will probably lose the plant; the pest is not particular to aloe water but unfortunately rather deadly to aloe plants. Put the plant in a plastic bag to prevent the mites from escaping, and discard it immediately.

A CLOUD OF FLIES RISES WHENEVER YOU WATER

Likely cause: Fungus gnats
Solution: Stop watering until the soil is completely dry

Gnats usually arrive when the plant is getting too much water, not enough sun,

or is planted in regular potting soil that stays moist for longer. These pests need moist soil to thrive. In fact, the adult flies are less of a problem than the larvae and infants that live in the soil, feeding off your plant's roots. Make changes to the light and type of potting soil as necessary, and keep the plant a little drier than usual for a few weeks while regularly scanning to make sure they don't come back. Use sticky traps or an insecticidal spray to control the outbreak.

The soil around the plant is likely also infested, so this is a good opportunity to repot your plant. Dispose of the soil and replace it with a fresh succulent blend. It can be hard to get rid of all the eggs in the soil, so you may need to transplant twice to take care of the problem.

DRYING OR DROPPING BOTTOM LEAVES

Likely cause: Overwatering, not enough light, pest infestation, or natural life cycles
Solution: Remove the leaves, check watering schedule and light source

Make sure your watering schedule is set accurately to water only when the plant is dry and that it is getting adequate light. Inside, you should remove the drying leaves to prevent pests like spider mites that like that dry, dusty environment. Outside, you can leave them alone or remove the leaves if you wish. That said, there may be no problem at all with a plant with drying leaves. Plants naturally drop leaves to make room for new growth and to create detritus, which decomposes and enriches the soil. Search your plants for pests and scrutinize your maintenance schedule to determine if you are properly caring for the plant.

BROWN MARKS ON THE TOPS OF THE LEAVES

Likely cause: Sunburn
Solution: Move the plant out of direct sunlight and reacclimate it

Succulents can get sunburned at times. That can happen when they are not acclimated to the sun or when there is a surprise heat wave. To acclimate a plant (aka "hardening it off"), expose it to a little additional brightness or heat each day, letting the process take two weeks so that the plant can develop a resistance on the outer edges of its flesh. If you notice a plant starting to get sunburned, or if you are just anticipating it, move it away from the direct sun. The burns won't heal, but your plant will eventually replace those leaves.

BLACK SPOTS ON THE LEAVES

Likely cause: Thrips
Solution: Prune infected flowers and leaves, spray with insecticidal soap or neem oil

Thrips are slender black bugs that feast on other bugs as well as the tasty parts of your plants, such as newly formed buds and leaves. You can sometimes identify them by black spots left by their feces on the plant. Use soap or oil to control the spread. Prune damaged parts of the plant.

Prune lightly, as major cutting may open the plant to further thrip infestation.

LEAVES AND BRANCHES ARE BEING EATEN

Likely cause: Some critter is chomping your plant
Solution: Create a physical barrier, such as fencing or chicken wire

It isn't easy to protect outdoor plants from hungry mouths. There are a variety of urban and rural animals (deer, squirrel, and raccoons, for instance) that love to chow down on your garden. You can use chicken wire to cover plants; many animals can't find a way past it to the yummy foliage. Start there and see if it solves the problem. You may have to seek more extreme remedies if your plants continue to be eaten, or maybe you'll decide you don't want to fight nature and move your succulent garden indoors.

HOLES AROUND THE PLANT PLUS WILTING LEAVES

Likely cause: Gophers or other underground beasts
Solution: Set species-appropriate traps or place cages around the roots

This can be another challenge for outdoor plants. There are a variety of animals that tunnel underground and eat root systems, such as gophers, mice, moles and voles. Trapping and removing them is the best solution. You can also use gopher-proof cages around the root systems whenever you plant, if you know your yard has these pests.

WET SPOTS ON THE STEMS OR LEAVES

Likely cause: Could be frost damage
Solution: Remove damaged plants and use frost cloth

With all the plants profiled, you'll find a hardy temperature that it can survive in. This doesn't mean it can live at that temperature for an indeterminate amount of time. Even frost-resistant plants may get damaged if they are in cold weather for an extended period of time. Unfortunately, most succulents will not recover from frost damage. If you see extensive wet or mushy parts on the plant after a cold spell, remove the damaged plants and put frost cloth over the rest. Consider moving container succulents indoors for the winter.

LEAVES ARE WILTED AND YELLOWING

Likely cause: Overwatering, underwatering, or pest infestation
Solution: Depends on the underlying cause; diagnose and treat accordingly

This is one of the biggest questions in the plant world. Why are my plant's leaves turning yellow? There are so many possibilities that people have devoted entire books to the cause. The good news is that your plant is telling you there is a problem. Check the soil. If it is dry, water more regularly. If it is very wet, don't water again until it gets dry. Check the leaves, top and bottom. Are there signs of bugs? If so, treat with insecticidal soap, neem oil, or rubbing alcohol. Perhaps everything looks good; there are no pests and you have a solid watering schedule. Maybe that is a sign that your plant is rootbound or that it has worked through all the nutrients in its soil, which means it needs to be transplanted. Maybe it is a natural aspect of the plant's life cycle and there are no problems at all, and your plant is going into dormancy for a few months. The more you can learn about your plant, the more you will be able to recognize the problem and apply a solution.

GLOSSARY

Areoles: Small, round, fleshy areas where spines, hair, leaves, and flowers grow from a cactus. Found only on cacti, not all succulents.

Bulbils: Little plantlets on the top edges of plant leaves

Caudex: The exposed root ball above the soil

Caudiciform: A type of succulent plant that stores water in a fat, rooty stem protruding from the soil in a lump called a caudex

Cladodes: Flattened segments grown consecutively along jointed stems with notches along their edges

Clumping: Forming a batch of the same plant from offsets

Cyathia: The little growth from which the flowers emerge that determines whether a plant is a male or female specimen

Dioecious: A plant that has either male or female flowers

Dormant: A state of nongrowth when a plant reserves its energy during harsh weather

Epicuticular Wax/Farina: A powdery substance that provides some natural protection from water evaporation and sunburn

Epiphyte/Epiphyllum: A plant that lives on other plants without feeding off them

Etiolation: This happens to plants when they are grown in no light or less than optimal light. The stems grow long, searching for the light, they drop bottom leaves, and their top leaves are smaller. It dramatically affects plants' appearances, especially if they normally grow in tight, low, compact rosettes.

Glochids: Little hairs or spines, generally barbed, that are often found on the areoles of cacti

Hens and chicks: A type of succulent that has a central mother plant that grows many baby plants. The chicks are also known as offsets.

Horticultural charcoal: A grade of charcoal used for water management and drainage control in succulent container gardens and especially important for terrariums

Leggy: Describes a plant that has an overly long stem, usually from growing toward faraway light, and results in raising its rosette up off the surface of the plant in a somewhat unattractive way

Monocarpic: Describes a plant that flowers once and then dies

Propagation: The process of growing new plants from an existing plant

Pumice: A volcanic rock that serves as a supplement in succulent soil mixes to improve water drainage

Sepals: The leafy portion of the plant outside of the developing flowers

Specimen plant: The central focus plant of a design or landscape

Stressed: A state of being that can occur when succulents are given less water, more sun or heat, or even more cold than they normally like, and which brings out pink, red, and purple colors in the plants' flesh

Succulent: A plant that retains water in its leaves, stems, or roots

Terrarium: An ecosystem enclosed in glass

Variegated: A pattern of plant leaf color consisting of whites, creams, and yellows instead of the usual green

Vertical garden: A type of garden created to be hung and grown on a fence or wall

Xeriscape: A garden that grows and thrives with little or no irrigation

INDEX

ACKNOWLEDGMENTS

Thanks to Dan, Seth, Huckleberry, Sandy, William, Kris, Trudy, Moss, Molly, Zada, Ai, and Sydney, the truly special crew of Succulence, because our work communities matter, now more than ever.

Thanks to the glorious growers, marketers, sellers, and buyers of plants, whose deep love and care for the earth's flora is so critical, obvious, and true.

Thanks to everyone at Callisto Media for shepherding me through the writing of this book, and to Rachel Weill for excellent photography and Linda Lamb Peters and Ayla Trotman for brilliant photography support. Also, thanks to Allison Serrell, who set me on the literary path.

Thanks to my family and friends for love and support. Thanks to Amy, Trudy, Huckleberry, Cody, and Marble Halva for encouragement, strength, good humor, and love on the home front.

ABOUT THE AUTHOR

 **Ken Shelf** is the owner of Succulence, a garden and lifestyle store in San Francisco's Bernal Heights neighborhood. Ken's love for succulents began with a *Haworthia fasciata* he received as a gift in 1994, which he still has. Since then, Ken has been exploring the mighty power of succulents, their breathtaking beauty, and their incredible will to live. Over the past decade, he has taught numerous classes and workshops on succulents and vertical gardening. In addition, Ken creates masterful succulent centerpieces and arrangements for special occasions and provides custom landscaping and design work throughout the Bay Area. Ken and his wife, Amy, live in San Francisco with a variety of other humans, animals, and plants. Ken has also written a dozen plays, a novel he hopes to publish in 2022, and countless poems and song lyrics; he records music under the name K-Fad; and he wrote, directed, and produced a feature film.

CPSIA information can be obtained
at www.ICGtesting.com
Printed in the USA
JSHW010826100622
26799JS00002BA/5